Sue Warden

CREATIVE DECOR

Sue Warden

CREATIVE DECOR

WINDING
STAIR
PRESS

National Library of Canada Cataloguing in Publication Data
Warden, Sue
        Creative décor : beautiful and inspired projects for every room
ISBN 1-55366-065-X
1. Handicraft. 2. House furnishings. 3. Interior decoration accessories. I. Title.
TT157.W373 2001   745.5   C2001-901770-7

Cover design: Darrin Laframboise
Interior design: Sharon Foster Design
Front cover and interior photographs: Virginia MacDonald
Styling and propping: Carolyn Souch
Styling of bedding and linens: Midori Fujiwara
Cover photo: Make-up by Anne Rosenbloom
            Hair by Leslie MacKenzie, Head over Heels, Oakville, ON

Although every effort has been made to ensure the accuracy of the material included in this book, neither the author nor the publisher is responsible or liable in the event of misrepresentation of instructions or product application.

Winding Stair Press
An imprint of Stewart House Publishing Inc.
Etobicoke, Ontario
www.stewarthousepub.com
Executive Vice President and Publisher: Ken Proctor
Director of Publishing and Product Acquisition: Joe March

1   2   3   4   5   05   04   03   02   01

This book is available at special discounts for bulk purchases by groups or organizations for sales promotions, premiums, fundraising and educational purposes. For details, contact: Peter March, Stewart House Publishing Inc., Special Sales Department, 290 North Queen Street, Etobicoke, Ontario (416) 695-1361.

Printed and bound in Canada

To my husband, Martin,
and my son, Nicholas,
the loves of my life.

Contents

CHAPTER TWO

The Dining Room ... 33

CHAPTER ONE

The Kitchen ... 7

CHAPTER THREE

The Family Room ... 47

Special Thanks to the Following Companies
for their Corporate Support

DecoArt™

FISKARS®

WALNUT HOLLOW

Winward

ACKNOWLEDGEMENTS

This book was created with the help of a great many very talented and wonderful people and companies. I could not have accomplished this project without the support and encouragement of my friends, family and business colleagues. I am very grateful to all of them.

Many thanks to the companies who provided corporate sponsorship and product support for this book, and to the people who believed in me and gave me their support. Thanks to Stan Clifford, Etta Brown and all my friends at DecoArt. Thanks to Michelle Lahman at Fiskars Canada, Inc.; to my special friends, Henriette Lussier and André Boivin at Offray Ribbon Canada Inc.; to Carol Graf and Marilyn Vanderpan at Walnut Hollow and to Allan Shaw and Cathy Aylard at Domcord Belding; and to my friend at Winward A Lifestyle Company, Steve Baumgartner. Working with you all was more than just a business relationship.

Special thanks to my friend Sandra Nash, of SaMi's Custom Window Coverings, for the beautiful window treatments throughout the house. Your special talent made a house a home. And to Designer Fabric Outlet for providing the fantastic array of fabric Sandra used to create the spectacular windows. Thanks also to Catherine Caple for the beautiful upholstery on the master bedroom chairs. It is the combination of everyone's efforts that makes this book so pleasing to the eye.

A big thanks to Macmillan Canada, from everyone in marketing and sales, publicity, administration and creative, to Nicole de Montbrun, my very special friend, who has been supportive of this project from the very beginning. Without your constant encouragement, I fear this project may have gone by the wayside. I am very grateful to have worked with you and value your friendship. Special thanks to Robert Harris, Donna Brown, Sharon Foster and Anna Stancer for their support.

Certainly, without beautiful photography, this project would not be what it is, and I would like to especially thank Virginia MacDonald for her incredible talent. The photographs are what tell the story. Thanks to Carolyn Souch for the beautiful accents.

I am grateful to my friends and partners at Life Network and LMNOP Productions Inc. and to all involved in making my show the success that it is. "Sue Warden CraftScapes" has given me the opportunity to share my expertise with a great many people. It has opened the door and given me the freedom to follow my heart and pursue this project, which has been a passion of mine for so many years. I thank you for your support.

To Barb Caplan, my mentor, business advisor, lawyer and friend. Barb, I cannot tell you how much I appreciate your constant support and advice. Thanks also to Marion Hebb, my literary lawyer, and Lilana Novakovich, my agent and friend. Your support and help has been much appreciated. Thanks to Leslie MacKenzie and Anne Rosenbloom for making me look "30ish" on the cover of the book.

To my good friend, Kim McIlwaine, whose talent, guidance and advice was a constant source of encouragement and inspiration. You continued to give me the strength to push forward, always there to pitch in whatever way you could. The studio is not the same when we are not working side by side.

Special thanks to my loving sister and friend, Marion, who shares my passion and excitement for both the craft and home decor industries and is always right there when there are deadlines to be met. To my mom and dad, who watch my show every day, sometimes twice, and are forever encouraging and supportive. Love ya!

I am grateful to my family and friends. Your encouragement and support is nothing short of invaluable, and make the hard work all worthwhile.

To my son, Nicholas, who I love dearly and who keeps me smiling and totally distracts me when I need it most, thank you bud!

And last but certainly not least, to my husband, Martin. I am overwhelmed when I try to express my gratitude for your wisdom, advice, support, encouragement, belief in me and most importantly, your friendship. I love you very much.

Introduction

Crafting and home decor are such a big part of my life. The enjoyment I get from making something myself is immeasurable. My greatest pleasure, however, has been the opportunity to share my ideas and expertise over the years with all of you. Through hands-on teaching and my television program "Sue Warden CraftScapes", I have experienced the thrill of entering your homes every day in the hopes of inspiring you with new and innovative projects.

A heartfelt project for me, this book is based on my own home and marries crafting and home decor, two of today's fastest growing industries. I have endeavoured to combine the two in a simple, yet effective, manner that enables all of us to introduce beautiful accessories into our homes. Creative Decor provides you with 50 projects. Each chapter contains several projects created especially for a particular room of the house. Every project is accompanied by a list of materials, hints and tips to help you along the way, comprehensive, easy-to-follow instructions and beautiful photographs.

Designed to appeal to any skill level, the details that enhance many of the projects are often achieved using stencils, rubber stamps and simple paint techniques, which will attract both the beginner and the more seasoned enthusiast. Each project is carefully constructed to create a professional result. I have taken great care to keep the cost of each project reasonable and the instructions simple. My mandate for this book is to help you make beautifully elegant projects for your home.

As the do-it-yourself and home decor industries grow by leaps and bounds every year, the products available become not only more sophisticated, but more user-friendly as well. We are now able to achieve incredibly professional results with less time and work. Gone are the days when you had to be a professional artist to create something extra special for your home. The availability of instruction books, along with the explosion of "how-to" television programming, has opened the door to everyone. My hope is that you are inspired and, most of all, that you enjoy this gift to you.

Sincerely,
Sue

Commonly Used Tools

Glue Sticks

Glue Gun

Floral "U" Pins

Floral Picks

Floral Tape

Floral Wire

Painter's Tape

Large Stencil Brush

Medium Stencil Brush

Stencil Tape

Small Stencil Brush

Fan Brush

Flat Wash Brush

#10 Flat Brush

#12 Flat Brush

Angular Brush

Script Brush

Liner Brush

Multi-Purpose
Scissors

Softouch Sewing
Scissors

X-ACTO
Knives

Craft Snips

Sea
Sponges

Fine Grit
Sandpaper

Stencil
Spouncers

Palette Knife

Foam Paint Brush

Foam Paint Roller

CHAPTER ONE

The Kitchen

The kitchen is a great place to be. We work to create a warm atmosphere because, as we all know, family and friends flock to the kitchen, no matter what we do to keep them out! There must be a reason for this, so let's add our own personal touch to the room we spend so much time in. This chapter gives you some great ideas to add charm and warmth to that family gathering spot, introducing lots of creative yet simple projects. Decorate a clock using découpage or try your hand at making functional trivets, funky placemats and vibrant, colourful floral arrangements. Whether you are using paint, fabric or silk flowers, you'll be inspired and love every creative moment. My kitchen is full of bright and exciting colours, so it was easy to introduce lots of wonderful projects. Use your imagination and coordinate the colours with your own decor to make your kitchen a happy place.

Twelve Little Pictures

Materials Required:

- 12 small picture frames approximately 5 x 7 inches (12.5 cm x 17.75 cm) with a 3½-inch x 5½-inch (9-cm x 14-cm) opening
- DecoArt Americana acrylic paints:
  1 bottle Honey Brown
  1 bottle DeLane's Deep Shadow
  1 bottle Dried Basil Green
  1 bottle Avocado
  1 bottle Antique Gold
  1 bottle Lamp Ebony Black
- 1 gold pigment ink pad
- several small decorator rubber stamps, motif of your choice
- 1 small tube Burnt Umber oil paint
- 1 small tin linseed oil
- 1 bottle matte acrylic varnish or 1 can matte spray varnish
- fine grit sandpaper
- 1-inch (2.5-cm) wash paintbrush
- 3/8-inch (9-mm) angular paintbrush
- #12 shader paintbrush
- pencil
- ruler
- paper towel
- soft cloths
- water container

Instructions:

1. Remove the glass and backing cardboard from the frames. Sand all frames down well, removing any dust particles with a damp paper towel.

2. Lay the frames out in the pattern you wish to hang them on your wall.

3. Using the shader paintbrush, paint the front and edges of two frames Honey Brown, one frame DeLane's Deep Shadow, one frame Dried Basil Green, one frame Avocado and one frame Antique Gold. Allow the front and edges of each frame to dry and paint the back the same colour. Allow all paint to dry thoroughly. Apply a second coat, allowing the paint to dry.

4. Vary the design of the next frame by painting one side of the front of the frame with the DeLane's Deep Shadow, one side with Antique Gold, one side with Avocado and one side with the Dried Basil Green. Allow the first coat to dry and apply a second coat. Let it dry. Paint the back of the frame a solid colour, and let it dry. Follow the same steps for three more frames, mixing the colour combinations up. Allow all paint to dry thoroughly.

5. The last two frames will have a harlequin pattern to give the grouping of pictures some interest. Paint two frames, front and back, with the Dried Basil Green as a base coat. Allow the paint to dry thoroughly.

6. Using the pencil and ruler, draw a triangle from edge to edge, starting at the upper left-hand corner of the front of the frames. The size of the triangles depends on the size of your frames, as well as the look you wish to achieve. Continue the triangle pattern on all the sides and edges of the frames. The triangles do not have to be perfectly even. The more whimsical the design, the better.

7. Paint the triangular patterns, using the angular paintbrush. Vary the colours to avoid having two triangles of the same colour together. Include black in the pattern as well. Allow the paint to dry thoroughly.

8. Mix a small amount of the Burnt Umber oil paint and linseed oil. Dip a dry soft cloth into the mixture and rub it over the front and sides of all the frames to create an antique effect. Allow the oil to dry for 5 minutes, then gently wipe again with a second cloth. Let all frames dry overnight.

9. Apply a coat of the acrylic varnish, either by brushing lightly or using a spray. Allow the first coat to dry thoroughly and apply a second coat. Allow to dry.

10. Meanwhile, use the wash paintbrush to paint the cardboard backings of all the frames. Vary the colour of each backing. Allow the paint to dry.

11. Using the gold pigment ink pad and rubber stamps, apply various designs on the painted side of each of the backing cardboard pieces. Allow the ink to dry completely.

12. Decide which frame will go with which backing card. Again, vary the colours for interest.

13. Assemble the frames and lay them out close together on the floor. When you are satisfied with the arrangement, hang them on the wall.

Wooden Cookbook Holder

Materials Required:

- 1 wooden magazine box
- ½ yard (0.5 m) textured wallpaper
- 1 yard (1 m) Offray 1½-inch (4-cm) sheer ribbon to coordinate with paint colours
- DecoArt Americana acrylic paints:
  1 bottle Light Avocado
  1 bottle Reindeer Moss Green
  1 bottle Golden Straw
- 1 can matte acrylic spray varnish
- 1 1-inch (2.5-cm) wash paintbrush
- 1 large UHU glue stick
- glue gun and glue sticks
- fine grit sandpaper
- Fiskars 8" Multi-Purpose Scissors
- pencil
- water container
- paper towel

Instructions:

1. Using the sandpaper, gently sand the inside of the magazine box. Wipe any dust particles away with damp paper towel.

2. Trace the four sides of the magazine box onto the wrong side of the wallpaper using the pencil. Cut out each piece, keeping track of which side of the box they correspond to.

3. Using the glue stick, apply a liberal amount of glue to one side of the box.

4. Match up the appropriate wallpaper piece. Apply glue to the wrong side of the wallpaper piece and, making sure the wallpaper matches evenly with the side of the box, stick the wallpaper to the box. Press it firmly in place. Repeat on the other three sides. Allow the glue to dry overnight.

5. Apply a small amount of Light Avocado paint on the upper area of one side of the box. Do not cover the box entirely with the paint. Without washing the paintbrush, apply a small amount of the Golden Straw paint slightly below the green. Repeat with the Reindeer Moss Green. Keep repeating the paint colours until you are at the bottom of the box.

6. Dip the paintbrush into the water and blot slightly on the paper towel. Begin applying small amounts of water to the paint on the box, moving the paint around with the brush to create a "watercolour" or "washed" appearance. The colours will blend together. If you add too much water, the colours become muddy. Blot the entire side with a single sheet of paper towel.

7. Repeat steps 5 and 6 with the other three sides and allow all paint to dry thoroughly.

Wash the paintbrush and blot it dry with paper towel.

8. Apply two to three coats of any one of the three colours of paint to the inside of the box, allowing drying time between each coat. You may want to alternate the colours if you are making more than one box.

9. Paint the bottom of the box with the same colour as the inside. Allow all paint to dry thoroughly. Wash the paintbrush and blot it dry on paper towel.

10. In a well-ventilated area, spray the box inside and out with two to three coats of the spray varnish, allowing each coat to dry completely.

11. Cut the ribbon in half. Using the glue gun, attach one piece to each side of the back panel of the box, approximately 3 inches (8 cm) from the bottom. Tuck in the cut edge before gluing for a finished look.

12. Draw the two pieces of ribbon together and tie a shoelace bow.

HINTS, TIPS & GREAT THINGS TO KNOW:

The trick I've found with acrylic paint and water is to let myself go and not worry about the outcome. Most times, the results are quite beautiful, and if not, it's only paint! Try mixing different colours. You will amaze yourself with how easy "watercolour" really is.

Decoupaged Kitchen Clock

Materials Required:

- 1 7-inch (17.75-cm) square Walnut Hollow Solid Wood Clock
- 1 Walnut Hollow Clock Movement #TQ700P for ¾-inch (2-cm) clock face
- DecoArt Americana acrylic paints:
  1 bottle Sand
  1 bottle Georgia Clay
  1 bottle Dried Basil Green
- 1 bottle gloss acrylic varnish
- 1 UHU glue stick or white craft glue
- 1 roll KleenEdge painter's tape
- 1 package Anita's Hand-Painted Decoupage Prints—Garden & Herbs #16058
- 1 small foam paintbrush
- 1 small flat paintbrush
- small sharp scissors
- fine grit sandpaper
- water container
- paper towel
- 1 finishing nail

Instructions:

1. Sand the clock well and remove any dust particles with a damp paper towel.

2. Cover the edges of the clock with painter's tape. Use the small foam paintbrush to apply a coat of the Sand paint to the top of the clock. Allow the first coat to dry and apply a second coat. Allow the paint to dry thoroughly. Wash the paintbrush and blot it dry with paper towel.

3. Tape off the top of the clock, leaving the edges exposed.

4. Use the small flat paintbrush to apply a coat of the Georgia Clay paint to the first level of the edge and a coat of the Dried Basil Green paint to the second level of the edge. Allow the first coat to dry and apply a second coat. Paint the back of the clock with the Georgia Clay paint. Wash the paintbrush and blot it dry with paper towel.

5. Gently sand the edges of the clock to give it a distressed look. Gently sand the top to achieve a smooth, clean surface. Remove all dust with a damp paper towel.

6. Cut the decoupage prints you wish to use. Design the picture on the face of the clock before you begin to glue.

7. Glue the prints to the top of the clock. If using a glue stick, be sure not to smear any of the glue on the wood surface or on the front of the decoupage prints or the varnish will not adhere. Allow the glue to dry.

8. Use the foam paintbrush to apply coats of the gloss varnish to the top and sides of the clock. Allow drying time between each coat. Apply at least 15 coats of varnish in order to prepare the clock for the next step.

9. Use fine grit sandpaper to gently sand the top surface of the clock. Apply another two to three coats of varnish, allowing drying time between each coat.

10. Repeat step 9 until you have a smooth finished surface. Varnish the back of the clock and allow the varnish to dry completely.

11. Assemble the clock movement according to instructions. Attach the clock to the wall with a small finishing nail.

HINTS, TIPS & GREAT THINGS TO KNOW:

What should a beautiful decoupage project look like? The idea behind decoupage is to have the image on your project appear as though it were hand painted. Although this process takes a little more time and patience, the results are second to none and worth the extra effort. Try it on a small piece, like this clock, before moving on to larger projects.

Spring Table Arrangement

Materials Required:

- ❖ 1 large block Sahara floral foam
- ❖ 1 oblong container approximately 12 x 14 inches (30 cm x 35 cm)
- ❖ assortment of Winward Silks flowers:
  - 2 stems Orchids with multiple blooms
  - 5 to 6 stems Sweetpea
  - 2 stems large Lilies with buds
  - 3 stems large open Roses
  - 3 stems Alstroemeria
  - 2 stems Iris with one bloom each
  - 3 stems berries

- ❖ 1 small bag Spanish or sheet moss
- ❖ 1 small bag floral "U" pins
- ❖ floral knife
- ❖ glue gun and glue sticks
- ❖ Fiskars Craft Snips
- ❖ Fiskars 8" Multi-Purpose Scissors

Instructions:

1. Use the floral knife to cut the corners of the floral foam to fit the container. Glue the foam into the container securely.

2. Using the Craft Snips, cut one stem of orchids to approximately 8 inches (20 cm). Insert and glue the orchid stem into the foam so the flowers cascade down the right side of the container.

3. Fill in around the orchids with 1 to 2 stems of smaller flowers, such as sweetpea, keeping the lengths of the flowers approximately the same.

4. Cut one lily stem to approximately 6 inches (15 cm). Insert and glue the lily to the left side of the arrangement. Alongside the lily, towards the middle front of the arrangement, glue a large rose, keeping the length of the flower stems even.

5. On the opposite side of the arrangement insert and glue another large lily as well as a rose.

6. Glue a full stem of alstroemeria in the middle of the arrangement. Keep the alstroemeria low, around 6 inches to 8 inches (15 cm to 20 cm) from the foam.

7. Insert and glue one single iris alongside the alstroemeria and another iris to the right of the arrangement.

8. Insert and glue another rose to the right of the arrangement, alongside the cascade of orchids.

9. Fill in the arrangment with any leftover flowers. Keep the larger flowers low and keep the whole design oblong, blending colours as you go.

10. Insert and glue sprigs of berries throughout the arrangement.

11. Fill in areas around the outside rim with small pieces of moss, using "U" pins to hold the moss in place. If you wish, you can add a bow.

HINTS, TIPS & GREAT THINGS TO KNOW:

Look around your house for a container. The container I used is an old floral dish of my mother's. I simply repainted it to give it a whole new look.

Go with a multitude of spring colours. Remember, everything in nature goes together. This arrangement will be seen from all sides, so make sure you turn your container often to keep the shape even.

Sword Fern Floor Cloth

Materials Required:

❖ vinyl or cushion flooring
(one piece cut 6 x 6 feet/2 m x 2 m)

❖ DecoArt Americana acrylic paints:
2 bottles Antique White
1 bottle Buttermilk
1 bottle DeLane's Deep Shadow
2 bottles Georgia Clay
1 bottle Burnt Umber
1 bottle Avocado
1 bottle Light Avocado
1 bottle Leaf Green
1 bottle Antique Gold

❖ 1 Buckingham Sword Fern stencil

❖ 1 Buckingham Terra Cotta Pots stencil

❖ 1 stencil roller

❖ 1 stencil roller refill

❖ 2 cans matte acrylic spray varnish

❖ 1 large bottle white gesso

❖ 1 permanent black marker

❖ 1 large sea sponge

❖ 1 medium stencil brush

❖ 1 roll KleenEdge painter's tape

❖ 1 roll stencil tape

❖ pencil and eraser

❖ quilter's ruler or yardstick

❖ X-Acto knife

❖ water container

❖ paper towel

Instructions:

1. Lay the piece of vinyl flooring on a flat working surface, wrong side up. Several tables pushed together work well.

2. Measure an even amount across each corner and cut the corners off using the X-Acto knife. The amount you cut off depends on the look you wish to achieve. You will now have a six-sided piece of vinyl.

3. Use the stencil roller to apply a coat of gesso to the entire surface. Allow the gesso to dry completely. Wash the stencil roller and blot it dry with paper towel.

4. Using a clean roller refill, apply two coats of the Antique White acrylic paint, allowing the first coat to dry before applying the second coat. Wash the roller refill and blot it dry with paper towel.

5. Mix some of the Buttermilk paint with a little water. Use a damp sea sponge to dab the paint gently all over the surface of the floor cloth. Allow the paint to dry. Wash the sea sponge and blot it dry with paper towel.

6. Use the ruler to find the centre of the floor cloth and make a light mark with a pencil at the middle point. Measure 1 inch (2.5 cm) on either side of the pencil mark and make two more marks. Erase the first pencil mark.

7. Find the middle of the bottom of the first Buckingham Terra Cotta Pot stencil. Line this point up with one of the pencil marks. Hold the stencil in place with the stencil tape.

8. Apply the DeLane's Deep Shadow paint to a clean stencil roller. Roll onto paper towel to remove some of the paint. Roll the stencil roller over the pot stencil. Repeat the same process for the second pot, so that it faces in the opposite direction. Wash the stencil roller and blot it dry with paper towel.

9. Place the second part of the pot stencil on top of the first stencilled design and apply the Georgia Clay paint colour for a shadowing effect. Following the instructions on the stencil packaging, go back in with a little Burnt Umber on your stencil brush to darken and shade the sides of the pot and any areas you think should be shaded. Wash and blot dry all tools.

10. Using a clean stencil roller and the Buckingham Sword Fern stencil, stencil leaves coming out of both pots. Vary the shades of green and stencil some leaves darker than others, using the Avocado, Light Avocado and Leaf Green paints to resemble natural plant colouring. Wash and blot dry all stencilling tools.

11. Draw a pencil line 6 inches (15 cm) in from the edge of each side of the floor cloth. Place painter's tape along the pencil lines and apply two to three coats of the Georgia Clay paint between the tape and the edge using a stencil roller. Allow drying time between coats. Wash and blot dry all stencilling tools.

12. Remove the tape and measure 1½ inch (4 cm) in from the inside edge of the Georgia Clay border.

Tape a second border off which touches the first border and paint this area with the Antique Gold. Again, use two to three coats of paint, allowing drying time between each coat. Wash and blot dry all stencilling tools.

13. Remove the tape and use the ruler and black marker to enhance the line between the borders and along the inside edge of the Antique Gold border. Allow everything to dry thoroughly.

14. Apply several coats of the matte spray varnish, allowing each coat to dry before applying the next. Allow the floor cloth to cure for a least one week before using.

Painting floor cloths used to intimidate me. I had never had an opportunity to investigate making this process easier. But I have since discovered that using vinyl flooring is not only inexpensive, but it's also extremely easy to handle. This floor cloth is rather large; however, it's no more difficult than making a smaller one. The only difference is, of course, you need a little more room. I love getting out in my garage in the spring and summer to start working on some of my larger projects. Enjoy!

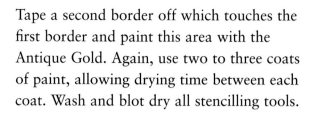

Harlequin Recipe Box

Materials Required:

- 1 Walnut Hollow double recipe box
- DecoArt Americana acrylic paints:
  1 bottle Yellow Ochre
  1 bottle Dried Basil Green
  1 bottle Ebony Lamp Black
- 1 bottle matte acrylic varnish
- 1 Plaid mini alphabet stencil
- 1 narrow roll KleenEdge painter's tape
- 1 roll stencil tape
- 1 1-inch (2.5-cm) flat paintbrush
- 1 small stencil brush
- fine grit sandpaper
- ruler
- pencil
- water container
- paper towel

Instructions:

1. Using the fine grit sandpaper, sand the recipe box well and remove all dust particles with damp paper towel.

2. Use the flat paintbrush to apply two to three coats of the Yellow Ochre paint to the inside and outside of the box. Allow drying time between each coat. Wash the paintbrush and blot it dry on paper towel.

3. Measure the edges of the top of the box to find the centre of each edge. Make a small pencil mark. Apply a piece of painter's tape from mark to mark to create a diamond shape on the top of the box. Press tape firmly in place.

4. Apply two coats of the Dried Basil Green paint inside the diamond shape, allowing drying time between each coat. Remove the tape. Wash the paintbrush and blot it dry with paper towel.

5. Repeat steps 3 and 4 for all sides of the box, ensuring the lid of the box is firmly in place while working so the points of all diamonds meet on all edges of the box. Allow drying time between each coat of paint.

6. Apply two to three coats of the acrylic varnish to the entire box, allowing drying time between each coat. This step makes it easy to do a quick cleanup if you make a mistake with the stencil.

7. Think out your stencilled design carefully. Use the stencil tape to hold your stencil in place. Using the small stencil brush and such a small amount of black paint that the brush is almost dry, pounce the paint onto the stencil. Spell the word "recipes" all over the box in any areas you wish.

8. Apply two more coats of varnish to the outside of the box, allowing drying time between each coat.

Placemats with a Twist

Materials Required:

- 6 pieces of linoleum or cushion flooring, each measuring approximately 15 x 20 inches (37.5 cm x 50 cm)
- DecoArt Americana acrylic paints:
  1 bottle Antique White
  1 bottle Buttermilk
  1 bottle Georgia Clay
  1 bottle Avocado
- 1 can matte spray varnish
- 2 small sea sponges
- 1 small foam paintbrush
- 1 wide-tipped gold paint pen

- 1 roll narrow KleenEdge painter's tape
- 1 roll wide KleenEdge painter's tape
- 1 small Rubber Stampede stamp of your choice
- 1 gold ink stamp pad
- X-Acto knife
- Fiskars 8" Multi-Purpose Scissors
- pencil
- ruler
- paper towel
- water container
- paper for making a pattern

Instructions:

1. Decide on the size and shape of your placemat. Measure properly to ensure it is even. Trace the pattern onto a sheet of paper in pencil, and cut it out. Use the pattern to cut the linoleum or cushion flooring with scissors or an X-Acto knife.

2. Turn the cut placemats over and paint the wrong side of the linoleum with a coat of the Antique White paint, using the foam paintbrush. (The "right" side of the linoleum becomes the underside of the placemat.) Allow the paint to dry. Wash the paintbrush and blot it dry on paper towel.

3. Using a damp sea sponge, dab the Buttermilk paint all over each placemat to create a mottled look. Allow the paint to dry completely. Wash the sponge and blot it dry on paper towel.

4. Measure the width of one placemat to find the centre. Run a strip of the wide painter's tape down the middle of the placemat from top to bottom. Leave one width of the painter's tape open and apply another strip of the tape parallel to the first strip, leaving a gap the same width as the tape. Repeat until the entire placemat is covered, taking care to keep the lines of your tape straight.

5. Sponge the Georgia Clay paint onto the open areas of the placemat. Remove the tape and allow it to dry.

6. Repeat the same process with the stripes running perpendicular, using the same colour. Allow all paint to dry. Wash the sponge and blot it dry on paper towel.

7. Use the narrow painter's tape to create narrower stripes in between the clay-coloured stripes in one direction. Make sure you tape off any areas that you do not want to paint.

8. Sponge the Avocado paint onto the open areas and let the paint dry. Remove the tape. Repeat with the stripes running perpendicular.

9. Use the gold paint pen and the ruler to draw lines down the middle of the clay-coloured stripes in both directions.

10. Stamp a gold design on every second intersection of clay-coloured stripes using the gold ink stamp pad and rubber stamp. Allow the stamp ink to dry completely. Repeat to make six placemats.

11. Spray all placemats with a coat of matte spray varnish. Allow the first coat to dry and apply a second coat. Allow all varnish to dry thoroughly.

HINTS, TIPS & GREAT THINGS TO KNOW:

You can enjoy painted plaid designs in any area of your home. This method works very well on small wall areas, and looks great on a floor cloth. When making these placemats, keep in the mind the shape of your table. I have a round table in my kitchen, and therefore I cut the placemats to accommodate.

Decorative Trivits

Materials Required:

- Walnut Hollow wooden star, octagon and quilt block trivets
- DecoArt Americana acrylic paints:
  1 bottle Camel
  1 bottle Williamsburg Blue
  1 bottle DeLane's Dark Flesh
  1 bottle DeLane's Deep Shadow
  1 bottle Avocado
  1 bottle Napa Red
  1 bottle Antique Gold
- 1 Plaid Simply Stencils Decorator Backgrounds, pattern of your choice
- 3 4- x 4-inch (10-cm x 10-cm) ceramic tiles in black or colour of your choice
- 1 tube Burnt Umber oil paint
- 1 small tin linseed oil
- 1 tube Crafter's Goop
- 1 carton Plaid Make-It Mosaics tile grout
- 1 roll stencil tape
- 2 to 3 small stencil brushes
- 1 small foam paintbrush
- 1 palette knife
- 1 bottle matte acrylic varnish
- 1 small sea sponge
- fine grit sandpaper
- soft cloths
- paper towel
- water container

Instructions:

1. Using the sandpaper, sand all the trivets well, removing any rough edges. Remove all dust particles with damp paper towel.

2. With the small foam paintbrush, paint two coats of the Camel acrylic paint on each trivet, allowing drying time between each coat. Wash the paintbrush and blot it dry with paper towel.

3. Decide on which stencil design you wish to place on each trivet. Use the stencil tape to hold the stencil in place.

4. To apply the first design, dip one stencil brush in a small amount of one of the acrylic paints. Blot most of the paint off the brush onto paper towel. Begin applying the paint to the stencil in a pouncing motion, working from the inside of the design out and making sure your paint is not too heavy. Continue this process, changing colours and brushes until the design on the top of the trivet is complete.

5. Repeat this process for the other two trivets, varying the design. Allow all the paint to dry. Wash all stencil brushes and blot them dry on paper towel.

6. Use the small foam paintbrush to apply a light coat of acrylic varnish to each trivet, front and back. Allow the varnish to dry. Wash the paintbrush and blot it dry.

7. Mix a small amount of the Burnt Umber oil paint with a small amount of linseed oil. Mix well.

8. Use a soft cloth to gently wipe a light coat of the mixture to all sides of each trivet. Allow the oil to dry for five minutes and use a second soft cloth to wipe away the excess. Allow the oil to dry overnight.

9. Use the foam paintbrush to apply another coat of the acrylic varnish to all trivets. Allow the varnish to dry thoroughly.

10. Following the manufacturer's instructions on the Crafter's Goop, insert and glue one tile into the tile area of each trivet. Allow the glue to dry completely.

11. Mix a small amount of Plaid Make-It Mosaics grout according to the manufacturer's instructions. Add a small amount of Camel acrylic paint to the grout.

12. Use the palette knife to push the coloured grout into the crack or groove around the edges of each tile. Wipe away all excess grout with the dampened sea sponge. Allow the grout to dry thoroughly.

HINTS, TIPS & GREAT THINGS TO KNOW:

Not only are these trivets very functional, they also make wonderful wall decorations when hung with plate hangers. This keeps them off your counter when you're not using them, and readily available when you need them. How about making a set as a house warming or shower gift?

Every kitchen needs a bulletin board to keep our lives in order, but it doesn't have to be a plain, purchased corkboard. Just a little fabric and paint will help make that functional piece a decorative accent to your room. This is a great opportunity to use the fabric already in your kitchen or any other room in your home. It also gives you an option of introducing a fourth and fifth fabric into the room.

Fabric Covered Bulletin Board

Materials Required:

- ❖ 1 cork bulletin board (approximately 22 x 16 inches/56 cm x 41cm)
- ❖ 1 yard (1 m) each of three different fabrics
- ❖ 3 yards (2.75 m) Domcord Belding flat decorative trim
- ❖ DecoArt Americana acrylic paint: 1 bottle DeLane's Deep Shadow
- ❖ DecoArt Americana gel stain: 1 bottle Walnut
- ❖ 1 small bottle matte acrylic varnish
- ❖ 1 1-inch (2.5-cm) flat paintbrush
- ❖ 12 to 14 upholstery tacks or decorative buttons
- ❖ sewing machine
- ❖ straight pins
- ❖ soft cloth
- ❖ glue gun and glue sticks
- ❖ Fiskars Softouch Multi-Purpose Scissors
- ❖ ruler
- ❖ water container
- ❖ paper towel

Instructions:

1. Cut ten 5½-inch (14-cm) squares from all three fabrics for a total of 30 squares. Increase the amount of squares in accordance with the size of corkboard purchased.

2. Arrange the squares on the floor so they form a diamond, alternating the squares in an even and pleasing manner.

3. Pin the squares together in strips, leaving approximately a ½-inch (1-cm) seam allowance. Sew each strip separately, lining up the seams. Sew all the strips together to form one large patchwork diamond. Set the fabric diamond aside.

4. Using the flat paintbrush, apply one coat of the DeLane's Deep Shadow paint to one side of the board's wooden frame. Immediately wipe the paint away with paper towel, leaving a "stained" effect. Repeat this process on the rest of the frame. Wash the paintbrush and blot it dry with paper towel.

5. With a soft cloth, gently apply a light coat of the gel stain over the frame of the board to darken the colour slightly. Allow everything to dry completely.

6. Use the paintbrush to apply two to three coats of acrylic varnish to the frame. Allow drying time between each coat.

7. Lay the fabric diamond right side up, onto the face of the bulletin board, so that the fabric covers the cork. Cut the fabric diamond to fit the inside of the board's frame and trim edges evenly.

8. Using the glue gun, run a small amount of glue around the edges of the cork and adhere the fabric to the board.

9. Glue the trim around the inside edges of the board to cover the raw edges of the fabric.

10. Push upholstery tacks into each intersection of the individual fabric diamonds, or glue on decorative buttons with the glue gun.

Mosaic Utensil Holder

Materials Required:

- 1 6-inch (15-cm) square Walnut Hollow planter box
- DecoArt Americana acrylic paint:
  1 bottle Lamp Ebony Black
  1 bottle Georgia Clay
- 4 4-inch (10-cm) black ceramic tiles
- 1 tube Crafter's Goop
- 1 bag black glass beads
- 1 carton Plaid Make-it Mosaics tile grout
- 1 bottle matte acrylic varnish
- 1 medium foam paintbrush
- disposable latex gloves
- palette knife
- hammer
- disposable plastic container
- soft cloths
- kitchen sponge
- heavy brown paper bag
- safety glasses
- water container
- paper towel

Instructions:

1. Using the medium foam paintbrush, paint the inside, upper rim and bottom of the planter box with two coats of the Lamp Ebony Black paint. Allow drying time between coats. Wash the foam paintbrush and blot it dry on paper towel.

2. Apply two to three coats of the acrylic varnish to the inside, upper rim and bottom of the planter. Allow the varnish to dry between coats.

3. Place one tile at a time into the brown paper bag. Wearing the safety glasses, tap the tile with the hammer until it breaks into small and medium-sized pieces. Repeat with each tile.

4. Using the Crafter's Goop, glue pieces of tile and glass beads onto the sides of the wooden planter, designing a pattern as you go. Make sure you are working in a well-ventilated area. Allow approximately ½ inch (1 cm) between each mosaic piece.

5. In a disposable container, mix the entire carton of tile grout with a small amount of water.

6. Mix the Georgia Clay paint into the grout with the palette knife until it is the consistency of thick mud.

7. Wearing the gloves, apply the grout to the sides of the planter over the glass beads and broken tile pieces. Ensure the grout is pushed well into the spaces between the tiles and glass beads. Follow the manufacturer's instructions and allow the grout to "set up" for approximately 15 minutes.

8. With a damp sponge, wipe the excess grout off the surface of the tiles and glass beads. You will have to repeat this step a few times, washing the sponge after each wipe. Make sure you remove all the excess. Once the grout is dry, you cannot remove it.

9. Allow the grout to dry overnight and buff the tiles and beads with a dry, soft cloth.

CHAPTER TWO

The Dining Room

How often do you actually use your dining room? Some people use theirs all the time and others just once in a while. My family fits somewhere in between. We love to entertain, but we are more of the outdoor-barbecue kind of people and enjoy relaxed, no-fuss meals and entertaining. I do, however, want my dining room to look elegant and sophisticated, with a comfortable, warm feel. I chose a little more formal window treatment in this room, and decided to decorate the walls with simple tapestries made from scraps of the same fabric used for the window treatment. It only takes small amounts of wonderful trims and tassels to turn any room into a work of art. I decided to focus on the table and pass on some great project ideas that everyone can do. As with most dining rooms, the table is the focus of the room and we want it to look wonderful all the time, not just when it is set for guests. I have created a great floral centrepiece that all can enjoy, an exquisite table runner and, of course, the beautiful silk napkins and jute napkin rings. These items are all essential to draw the eye to the table. The gilded candle box is a fabulous way to keep your candles organized.

Rustic Floral Design

Materials Required:

- 1 container approximately 14 to 16 inches (35 cm to 41 cm) in height
- assortment of Winward Silks flowers:
    7 stems celedon green Lilies
    6 stems burnt orange Cabbage Roses
    3 stems burnt orange Zinnias
    5 stems yellow/gold Zinnias
    6 stems burnt orange Lilac
    4 stems yellow/gold Cabbage Roses
    12 stems celedon green Ranunculus
- 2 large blocks Sahara floral foam
- 1 small bag sheet moss
- 1 small bag floral "U" pins
- floral knife
- Fiskars Craft Snips
- Fiskars Softouch Multi-Purpose Scissors
- glue gun and glue sticks

Instructions

1. Using the floral knife, cut the two foam blocks to fit snugly inside the container. Glue the foam in place, gluing one block on top of the other. Fill in the container with the left-over pieces of foam.

2. Cover the floral foam with the sheet moss, attaching it with the floral "U" pins.

3. Use the Craft Snips to cut one lily stem approximately one-and-a-half to two times the height of the container. Glue the lily into the middle of the arrangement.

4. Cut two more lily stems 2 inches (5 cm) shorter than the first. Insert and glue one stem on each side to create a triangular shape.

5. Cut the last four stems of lilies roughly 1 inch (2.5 cm) shorter again, gluing two each on either side of the first lily. This creates the base.

6. Cut one burnt orange cabbage rose slightly shorter than the first lily. Insert and glue this rose to one side of the lily.

7. Cut two burnt orange cabbage roses 2 inches (5 cm) shorter than the first. Insert and glue one on each side of the arrangement around the two parallel lilies. Glue the other three burnt orange cabbage roses inside the triangles, keeping the shape at all times.

8. Cut, insert and glue the eight zinnias throughout the arrangement, paying attention to the colours.

9. Cut the six lilac stems about the same length as the zinnias. Insert and glue two stems of lilacs so they protrude from the sides and glue the rest within the arrangement.

10. Stand back from the arrangement and look for any uneven areas or "holes" in the design. Use the four yellow cabbage roses to fill these areas.

11. Cut the ranunculus stems to fill in the open areas of the arrangement. Insert and glue all stems in place.

HINTS, TIPS & GREAT THINGS TO KNOW:

The beauty of this arrangement is not in how it is put together, but in the quality and colours of the flowers themselves. This is a very good example of a relatively simple arrangement made spectacular by spending a little more on very good-quality products. I chose these flowers for their colour appeal and the way they enhance my dining room; however, once again feel free to change the colours to complement your decor.

Designer Table Runner

Materials Required:

- two decorator fabrics, in sufficient quantity to cover the table
- lining fabric such as heavy-weight cotton
- 4-inch (10-cm) Domcord Belding bullion trim, in sufficient quantity to finish the table runner
- tailor's chalk
- thread
- sewing machine
- Fiskars Softouch Multi-Purpose Scissors
- straight pins
- measuring tape

Instructions:

1. Measure the table and decide on the finished length and width of the table runner. To determine the size of the centre panel of the runner, subtract two times the desired finished width of the border from the desired finished length and width of the runner. Add 1 inch (2.5 cm) to the length and width to allow for ½-inch (1-cm) seam allowances.

2. To make four border strips, cut two strips the length of the middle panel plus twice the width of the finished border. Add 1 inch (2.5 cm) for seam allowances. Cut two strips the width of the middle panel plus twice the width of the border. Add 1 inch (2.5 cm) for seam allowances. The width of the border strips should total the desired finished width plus 1 inch (2.5 cm) for seam allowances.

3. On the wrong side of the fabric, use the tailor's chalk to mark the centre of the middle panel on the sides and ends. Mark the centre of each border strip on the wrong side of the fabric.

4. Again, on the wrong side of the fabric, mark the middle panel ½ inch (1 cm) in from the raw edges on all corners.

5. With right sides together, pin one border strip to one side of the middle panel, matching raw edges and centres. Stitch, leaving ½-inch (1-cm) seam allowances starting and ending at corner markings. Repeat for all other border strips.

6. Match the border seams and raw edges of the border strips by folding the centre panel diagonally at one corner. Use a ruler and chalk and mark a 45° angle line along the fold to mitre the corners.

7. Pin and stitch the mitred seam, beginning at the raw edge and ending at the previous seamline. Trim seam allowances to ½ inch (1 cm). Repeat on all corners. Trim and press all seams open.

8. Cut lining ½-inch (1-cm) shorter on all sides than the runner. Pin it to the runner, right sides together, and stitch, leaving a ½-inch (1-cm) seam allowance on all sides. Leave an area open for turning.

9. Trim seam allowances, press all seams flat, turn right side out and hand stitch the opening closed.

10. Sew the bullion on to the right side of the ends of the runner.

HINTS, TIPS & GREAT THINGS TO KNOW:

I have written these instructions to give you the flexibility to make this table runner any size you wish. Dining room tables vary greatly in size. By taking the exact measurements of your table, you can make this runner perfect. My table runner is made from heavy designer fabric, the same fabric used for the window treatment in the room; however, there are so many beautiful decorator fabrics available that the choices are unlimited. Just be sure to use a fabric with good body to ensure satisfactory results.

Gilded Candle Box

Materials Required:

- 1 Walnut Hollow candle box
- 1 package Houston Art Copper Leaf
- 1 bottle Houston Art Gold Leaf Adhesive Size
- DecoArt Americana acrylic paint: 1 bottle Lamp Ebony Black
- 1 stencil of your choice
- 1 small tin linseed oil
- 1 small tube Burnt Umber oil paint
- 1 bottle matte acrylic varnish
- 1 1-inch (2.5-cm) flat paintbrush
- 1 small stencil brush
- 1 roll narrow KleenEdge painter's tape
- fine grit sandpaper
- pencil
- ruler
- paper towel
- soft cloth
- water container

Instructions:

1. Sand the box well and remove any dust particles with a damp paper towel.

2. Use the paintbrush to apply two coats of the Lamp Ebony Black paint to the entire box, inside and out. Allow drying time between each coat. Wash the paintbrush and blot it dry with paper towel.

3. Use the pencil and ruler to make a 1-inch (2.5-cm) border around the outside edge of the top of the box. Mask off the inside rectangle on the top of the box with the painter's tape.

4. Using the paintbrush, apply a coat of the adhesive size to all sides of the outside of the box. Allow it to dry at least one hour. It will be clear and tacky when dry. Wash the brush and blot it dry.

5. Gently begin laying sheets of the copper leaf onto the box, smoothing gently with a soft, dry paintbrush. Cover the box completely. Brush away any bits of leaf that do not adhere. Some of the black paint will show through to give an aged appearance.

6. Remove the tape from the inside rectangle on top of the box.

7. Centre the stencil design in the middle of the rectangle. Hold it in place with small pieces of painter's tape.

8. Using the small stencil brush, lightly dab the adhesive into the open areas of the stencil. Wash the stencil brush and blot it dry with paper towel. Remove the stencil and allow the adhesive to dry.

9. Apply copper leaf to the stencilled design.

10. Use the flat paintbrush to apply two coats of the acrylic varnish to the entire box, inside and out. Allow the varnish to dry thoroughly between coats.

11. With the soft cloth, apply a coat of linseed oil directly over the copper leaf on the outside of the box.

12. Apply a light rubbing of the Burnt Umber paint over the oil, using the same cloth. The oil and paint work together to create an aged effect on the leaf. Allow the oil and paint to dry overnight.

13. Once the oil and paint are dry, apply two to three coats of the varnish to the outside of the box, allowing drying time between coats.

HINTS, TIPS & GREAT THINGS TO KNOW:

Leafing comes in gold, silver and copper. Because I am drawn to gold, I tend to stay with one colour; however, I decided with this project to be a little daring and head towards the copper. When I finished the candle box, I noticed that the copper was very brilliant and beautiful, but I wanted to tone it down just a little so it would melt into the warmth of the room. To achieve this effect, I used my favourite antiquing method, a combination of linseed oil and Burnt Umber oil paint.

Faux Tapestries

Materials Required:

- 1 to 3 Walnut Hollow wooden picture frames, size of your choice
- scraps of tapestry fabric
- latex paint
- 1 bottle matte acrylic varnish
- heavy cardboard
- 1 1-inch (2.5-cm) flat paintbrush
- fine grit sandpaper
- Fiskars 8" Multi-Purpose Scissors
- X-Acto knife
- ruler
- pencil
- paper towel
- water container
- glue gun and glue sticks

Instructions:

1. Using the fine grit sandpaper, sand the picture frames well and wipe the dust particles away with a damp paper towel.

2. Use the flat paintbrush to apply a coat of the latex paint to the front of the frames and allow it to dry thoroughly. Turn the frames over and paint the back and sides. Allow the paint to dry well. Wash the paintbrush and blot it dry on paper towel.

3. Gently sand the front of the frames to give a distressed look. Wipe the dust particles away with damp paper towel.

4. Once you have distressed the front of the frames to your liking, apply two to three coats of the acrylic varnish to the front, back and sides of the frames, allowing drying time between each coat. Wash the paintbrush and blot it dry with paper towel.

5. Measure the opening of the picture frames with the ruler and cut one piece of heavy cardboard to fit snugly in each opening, using the X-Acto knife for a clean cut.

6. Cut pieces of fabric to cover each piece of cardboard. Wrap the cardboard neatly with the fabric and glue it in place.

7. Insert one piece of covered cardboard into each opening of the frames so the fabric motif shows from the front.

8. Mount the frames on the wall. If you are making more than one, ensure they are mounted evenly. I like to use a level to get my measurements exact.

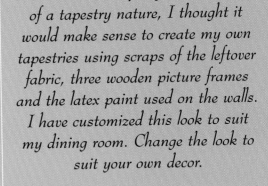

HINTS, TIPS & GREAT THINGS TO KNOW:

Sometimes our best project ideas come from simply starting with a piece of wood, a few paint colours and a bit of fabric. That's exactly what happened with this project. I wanted something different, but very simple, for one of the empty walls in my dining room. I thought about purchasing a tapestry, but I didn't want to spend a lot of money. Since my window treatment is fairly dramatic and of a tapestry nature, I thought it would make sense to create my own tapestries using scraps of the leftover fabric, three wooden picture frames and the latex paint used on the walls. I have customized this look to suit my dining room. Change the look to suit your own decor.

Silk Napkins and Jute Napkin Rings

Materials Required:

- 3 yards (2.75 m) patterned tablecloth fabric
- 2 yards (1.8 m) silk fabric
- coordinating thread
- 8 plastic plumbing join rings
- 1 bolt of jute twine
- 8 glass beads or decorative charms
- measuring tape
- Fiskars Softouch Multi-Purpose Scissors
- sewing machine
- iron and ironing board
- glue gun and glue sticks

Instructions:

1. Wash and dry the tablecloth fabric, using no fabric softener or dryer sheets. Iron the fabric flat.

2. With the measuring tape and scissors, measure and cut eight pieces of tablecloth fabric, each piece 22 x 22 inches (56 cm x 56 cm).

3. Repeat the same process with the silk fabric, cutting eight pieces that measure 20 x 20 inches (50 cm x 50 cm).

4. Using the straight stitch on the sewing machine, finish the sides of each piece of tablecloth fabric and each piece of silk

fabric by turning the edges over ¼-inch (6-mm) twice and stitching in place. Press all napkins flat.

5. Cut approximately 6 yards (5.5 m) of jute. Using the glue gun, apply a very small amount of glue to one end of the jute piece and glue it on the inside of one of the plumbing joins.

6. Begin wrapping the jute around the join, keeping the jute very close together to cover the black plastic. Continue until the piece is completely covered and glue the end down on the inside of the join. Repeat this process with the other seven joins to create eight napkin rings.

7. Glue a small glass bead to each napkin ring.

8. Place one silk napkin on top of one larger napkin. Pinch the fabrics in the middle and insert the napkins into the napkin rings. Repeat this process for the other seven.

HINTS, TIPS & GREAT THINGS TO KNOW:

This project is so simple, yet very elegant. The combination of silk fabric with jute shows real inspiration and lends itself to a very different and wonderful look. I love the effect of two different napkins, one acting as an overlay for the other. You can use the napkin made from the tablecloth fabric, which is very easy to keep clean, and leave the silk overlay as a decorative accent.

CHAPTER THREE

The Family Room

The family room is the heart of the home. It's a place where we can all gather together and spend time reading a good book, playing a game of cards or just relaxing in front of a warm fire on a cold winter night. I have endeavoured to introduce rich colour into this room, accenting the sofa and chairs with large, overstuffed designer pillows, which are easy to make and cost effective. I love whimsical floral designs that enhance elegantly stencilled end tables. For an added accent, try your hand at recycled coasters to complete the warm and friendly atmosphere. Create an inviting grapevine wreath, and don't forget a place to store all those decorating magazines. See you in front of the fireplace!

Romantic Flower Arrangement

Materials Required:

- ❖ 1 rectangular container approximately
  9 x 4½ x 4½ inches
  (23 cm x 11.5 cm x 11.5 cm)
- ❖ 4 yards (3.7 m) 1½-inch (4 cm) Offray
  floral ribbon
- ❖ 1 paddle 24–26 gauge floral wire
- ❖ 1 large block Sahara floral foam
- ❖ 1 small bag Spanish moss or sheet moss
- ❖ assorted dried flowers:
  2 packages burgundy Celosia or large
  dried flower
  2 packages Deliciosa or small filler bush
  2 packages purple preserved or dried Statice

- 1 package pink Larkspur
- 2 packages Parvafolio or Boxwood greenery
- 2 packages of natural Ti Tree
- 1 package preserved Salal Leaves
- 2 large Curly Willow branches
- ❖ 1 package of 2- or 3-inch (5-cm or 8-cm)
  wooden floral picks
- ❖ 1 package floral "U" pins
- ❖ 1 roll floral tape
- ❖ glue gun and glue sticks
- ❖ Fiskars Craft Snips
- ❖ Fiskars 8" Multi-Purpose Scissors
- ❖ Measuring Tape

Instructions:

1. Drizzle a small amount of glue into the bottom of the container. Push the entire block of floral foam firmly into the container.

2. Cover the top of the floral foam with a thin layer of moss. Use the floral "U" pins to hold it in place.

3. Begin in the middle of the arrangement. Measure approximately 18 inches (46 cm) up from the bottom of the container. This measurement will vary if you are using a different sized container.

4. Using the Craft Snips, cut one stem of celosia to reach this height and glue it into the middle of the foam.

5. Insert and glue four more celosia flowers on each side of the middle flower. Angle them outwards and use the Craft Snips to cut them slightly shorter than the first flower.

6. Insert and glue any remaining celosia throughout the arrangement. Remember the arrangement will be seen from all sides, so be sure to evenly distribute the flowers.

7. Insert and glue pieces of the deliciosa around the celosia, creating a rounded spray effect. Branch out to the sides of your arrangement and continue to check for evenness.

8. Once you have developed the shape, continue to fill in the arrangement with the rest of the deliciosa. Insert and glue pieces of the purple statice, keeping the middle pieces longer and shortening them as they get closer to the container.

9. Arrange the preserved greenery throughout. I used parvafolio; however, you can use boxwood or another small-leafed material. Repeat the same process with the larkspur and add long graceful pieces of ti tree.

10. Insert and glue or pin the salal leaves around the base of the arrangement to cover the moss and soften the look.

11. Glue the curly willow in the middle of the arrangement. These should be approximately 4 inches (10 cm) taller than all the other flowers. Be gentle!

12. Make a mini-loop bow with the ribbon and secure with a piece of wire. Glue the bow into the arrangement.

HINTS, TIPS & GREAT THINGS TO KNOW:

Before getting started, open your packages of flowers and separate the stems so you know exactly what you have. You may find some of the stems of the flowers are rather fragile. Try using a wooden floral pick to strengthen them: place the wooden pick alongside the stem and wrap the small piece of wire attached to the pick around the stem. Finish by wrapping floral tape down the stem of the flower over the wooden pick. The tape adheres to itself as you pull and wrap. This strengthens and lengthens your stem.

Stencilled Side Tables

Materials Required:

- 2 Walnut Hollow wooden oval end tables
- DecoArt Americana acrylic paint:
  1 bottle Plantation Pine
  1 bottle Hauser Medium Green
- 1 can Minwax Polyshades satin finish stain in Antique Walnut
- 1 Plaid Stencil Decor damask stencil
- 1 medium to large stencil brush
- 1 roll stencil tape
- several foam paintbrushes in various sizes
- 1 small bottle satin acrylic varnish
- soft cloths
- fine grit sandpaper
- fine steel wool
- water container
- paper towel
- carpenter's glue

Instructions:

1. Sand all pieces of both tables, either by hand using fine grit sandpaper, or a sanding tool. Follow the grain of the wood and wipe away any dust particles using a damp paper towel.

2. Using a medium foam paintbrush, begin applying the stain to the individual pieces of the tables, first staining the top of all pieces. Allow the stain to dry overnight. Stain the underside of each piece, and allow this coat to dry.

3. Gently rub both sides of all pieces with the fine steel wool. Remove any steel wool residue with a soft cloth.

4. Repeat step 2 to apply a second coat on all pieces. Allow the tables to dry thoroughly and again, rub them with fine steel wool. Remove any residue.

5. Dip the wooden plugs in a small amount of the stain. Move them around in the stain, removing them after 30 seconds. Allow them to dry. Wipe off any excess stain with a soft cloth.

6. Assemble the table according to the manufacturer's instructions. Allow any glue to dry, and apply the wooden plugs to the screw holes on both tables.

7. Centre stencil "A" on the top of one of the tables. Tape the stencil in place using the stencil tape.

8. Using the Hauser Medium Green paint, dip the stencil brush into the paint and blot it on paper towel. Begin pouncing the brush up and down on the stencil to fill in all open areas. Remove the stencil and repeat the same process on the second table while the first table is drying.

9. Using the colour indicators on the stencils, place stencil "B" on top of the pattern created by stencil "A" on the first tabletop. Tape stencil "B" in place. Pounce the Plantation Pine paint in the same manner to the open areas of the stencil. Remove the stencil and repeat this process on the second tabletop. Allow all paint to dry thoroughly.

10. Consider whether you wish to increase the number of images on the tabletop. If so, choose the appropriate parts of the stencil and follow the same procedure as steps 7 to 9.

11. Use a foam paintbrush to apply two to three coats of acrylic varnish to the tabletops only, allowing drying time between each coat.

HINTS, TIPS & GREAT THINGS TO KNOW:

There are several different types of one-step stains on the market these days. In other words, they contain the stain colour and the varnish protection all in one. They may take a little longer to dry, but the end result is a beautiful, rich tone on your wood piece and far less work. I needed new end tables for my family room, and found this was an easy, inexpensive and elegant way to go. Use any type of stencil you like on the top of the table to add that extra special touch. Be sure to protect the stencilled top with a few coats of extra varnish.

Painted Coasters

Materials Required:

- ❖ 6 old cork coasters
- ❖ DecoArt Americana acrylic paint:
  1 bottle Cranberry Wine
- ❖ DecoArt Americana Dazzling Metallics:
  1 bottle Glorious Gold
- ❖ 1 1-inch (2.5-cm) flat paintbrush
- ❖ 1 Plaid Stamp Decor decorator stamp,
  pattern of your choice
- ❖ 1 bottle gloss acrylic varnish
- ❖ fine grit sandpaper
- ❖ water container
- ❖ paper towel

Instructions:

1. Using the fine grit sandpaper, gently sand the top surface of the coasters and wipe away any dust particles with a damp paper towel.

2. With the flat paintbrush, apply a thin coat of the Cranberry Wine paint to each coaster. Allow the first coat to dry, and apply two to three more coats, allowing drying time between each coat.

3. Before applying the last coat of paint, give each coaster a gentle sand to remove any brush strokes or rough areas. Wipe the dust away with a paper towel and apply a final coat. Allow all paint to dry. Wash and blot the paintbrush dry on paper towel.

4. Use the paintbrush to apply a thin coat of Glorious Gold paint to the surface of the decorator stamp and place it in the middle of the first coaster. Gently push all areas of the stamp before removing. Repeat with the other five coasters. Allow all paint to dry. Wash the paintbrush and stamp and blot both items dry on paper towel.

5. When all paint is dry, apply two to three coats of the acrylic varnish, allowing drying time between each coat.

HINTS, TIPS & GREAT THINGS TO KNOW:

As time rolls on and your tastes and preferences change, you may find you have a few items stored away that you no longer use but just don't have the heart to throw away. That was the case with several old cork coasters I had in my basement. They were imprinted with botanical and bird images, which, in their day, were very pretty; however, I had outgrown them and wanted a change. By using a little paint, a stamp or two, and a bit of imagination, I turned my tired coasters into new, updated, functional items that will probably end up undergoing another facelift in years to come. If you decide to make these coasters, coordinate the paint colours with the decor of the room. I had the choice of cranberry, blueberry or forest green in my colour scheme. By the way, it's a good idea to practise using a stamp on a piece of paper towel before starting!

54

Designer Pillows

Materials Required:

- decorator fabric placemats and napkins
- fabric for pillow backings
- polyester fibrefill or pillow forms to fit placemat or napkin size
- tassels, four for each placemat pillow
- fringes, enough for each napkin pillow
- button cover kits in various sizes and refills, enough for two for each napkin pillow
- thread
- needle
- Fiskars Softouch Multi-Purpose Scissors
- sewing machine
- straight pins
- iron and ironing board

Placemat Pillow

Instructions:

1. Lay the placemat on the backing fabric, right sides together. Pin the placemat in place. Cut the backing fabric to the size of the placemat.

2. Pin a tassel to each corner of the right side of the placemat, leaving approximately ½ inch (1 cm) of the tassel ends.

3. With rights sides together, pin the placemat to the backing fabric, leaving an opening large enough to insert stuffing. Make sure you keep the tassels pinned in place and tucked between the placemat and backing.

4. Sew the placemat to the backing fabric, leaving a seam allowance of approximately ½ inch (1 cm). Reinforce the corners by using a

backstitch on the sewing machine to hold the tassels in place. Clip the corners, being sure not to clip the tassel ends too short.

5. Turn the pillow right side out, and press the edges neatly.

6. Stuff the pillow evenly with the polyester fibrefill, moving the stuffing well into the corners of the pillow.

7. Pin the opening closed and hand sew, using a small overstitch.

Napkin Pillows

Instructions:

1. Lay the napkin flat on the backing fabric, right sides together. Cut the backing fabric to the size of the napkin.

2. Match the nondecorative edge of the fringe to the edge of the napkin, right sides together, and pin the fringe in place. Machine stitch the fringe to the napkin.

3. With rights sides together, pin the backing fabric to the napkin, leaving an opening wide enough to insert a pillow form.

4. Sew the pieces together, clip corners and turn the pillow right side out. Adjust the fringe and press the edges neatly.

5. Insert the pillow form.

6. Pin and hand sew the opening closed.

7. Create two covered buttons using the backing fabric, following the manufacturer's instructions.

8. Use the needle and thread to make an indent in the middle of the pillow by pushing the needle through the middle to the other side, making a small stitch and pushing the needle back through to where you began. Tie the thread off tightly, leaving tails long enough to attach one covered button.

9. Slip one end of the thread through the shank of one button and tie it tightly to the pillow.

10. On the reverse side of the pillow, make thread loops by making a small stitch in the middle of the pillow, leaving the ends of the thread long. Attach the second button by the shank using the thread ends and tying them tightly.

HINTS, TIPS & GREAT THINGS TO KNOW:

These pillows look like I have spent hours quilting and designing, when in fact, I didn't. What I did was search out several coordinating fabric placemats and napkins that would group together nicely as pillows in the family room. The results were wonderful, as you can see, and the costs were kept to a minimum. I spent a little more on the placemats because I loved the pattern, colours and fabric, but I certainly did not spend as much as I would have had I purchased this type of pillow from a designer boutique.

Magazine Rack

Materials Required:

- ❖ 1 Walnut Hollow wooden magazine rack
- ❖ 1 small tin linseed oil
- ❖ 1 small tube Burnt Umber oil paint
- ❖ 1 home decor or rubber stamp
- ❖ 1 bottle acrylic paint, colour of your choice
- ❖ 1 can matte acrylic spray varnish
- ❖ 2 small foam paintbrushes
- ❖ palette paper
- ❖ several soft cloths
- ❖ fine grit sandpaper
- ❖ water container
- ❖ paper towel

Instructions:

1. Sand all the various wooden components of the magazine rack. Wipe away the dust particles with damp paper towel.

2. Using the small foam paintbrush, apply a generous layer of the linseed oil to one side of the first piece.

3. Squeeze a puddle of the oil paint onto palette paper. Dip a portion of a soft cloth into the oil paint. Gently rub the oil paint over the linseed oil, moving the paint around to cover the entire area. Wipe off any excess paint and oil with a clean soft cloth.

4. Repeat steps 2 and 3 on the remaining pieces of the magazine rack, front and back. Allow the oil to dry at least overnight.

5. Assemble the magazine rack, following the manufacturer's instructions.

6. Using the second small paintbrush, apply a layer of acrylic paint to the home decor stamp. Stamp the images on the outside of the rack, in a pleasing manner. When you are finished the design, wash the brush and stamp and blot them dry. Allow all paint to dry.

7. Once again using the linseed oil and Burnt Umber paint, apply a very thin layer of antiquing over the stamped design. Wipe away any excess. Allow everything to dry thoroughly.

8. Spray the entire magazine rack, inside and out, with two to three coats of varnish, allowing drying time between each coat.

Grapevine Wreath

Materials Required:

- 1 large grapevine wreath
- 3 large packages German Statice
- 5 yards (4.5 m) Offray 4-inch (10-cm) wired ribbon
- 24 to 26 gauge floral wire
- glue gun and glue sticks
- Fiskars Craft Snips
- Fiskars Softouch Multi-Purpose Scissors

Instructions:

1. Open the packages of German statice and separate the material into pieces approximately 6 inches (15 cm) in length.

2. Start at the bottom of the wreath and work up the right side, gluing pieces of material so that all pieces flow in the same direction. Each piece should overlap the previous one to fill the wreath completely.

3. Work the pieces along the outside and inside edges of the wreath as well, covering the grapevine. Leave a 4-inch (10-cm) opening at the bottom of the wreath.

4. Make a multi-loop bow with the ribbon, wiring the bow securely. Attach it to the open area at the bottom of the wreath using the wire and glue.

HINTS, TIPS & GREAT THINGS TO KNOW:

This wreath is a very simple arrangement, and a great starting point if you have not worked with dried material in the past. I wanted a large wreath, but I wanted to keep it very simple. The trick is to keep the German statice pieces going in the same direction all the way around the wreath and make the bow the focal area of the design.

CHAPTER FOUR

The Powder Room

I had a great time decorating my powder room. Once again, here was a small room that I could have a lot of fun with, and I did. Most of the time, I decorate by starting with one item that catches my attention and work from there. In this powder room, I started with the large homemade border. I found a wonderful colour print, purchased several copies of the same print, and decoupaged the cut prints evenly across the top of the room using a glue stick. I cut stars from the prints to create the lower border and incorporated the star motifs on some of the projects in the room. I chose functional objects, such as a wastebasket, a towel rack and a funky shelf. I used various textures to make my projects interesting, and accented the walls with inexpensive plaster pieces. A fabric picture montage finishes off a fun and funky room that creates a stir every time we have guests.

Ceramic Tile Shelf

Materials Required:

❖ 1 Walnut Hollow "Whatnot 3 Tile Shelf"
❖ DecoArt Sandstones:
  1 jar Neutral Beige
❖ DecoArt Americana acrylic paints:
  1 bottle Country Red
  1 bottle Baby Blue
❖ 1 jar DecoArt Decorating Paste
❖ 1 can gloss acrylic spray varnish
❖ 3 white 4-inch (10-cm) ceramic tiles
❖ 1 bottle Aleene's Thick Designer Tacky Glue
❖ 1 fan paintbrush
❖ 1 1-inch (2.5-cm) flat paintbrush
❖ 3 decoupage motifs of your choice
❖ 1 UHU glue stick
❖ several soft cloths
❖ Fiskars 8" Multi-Purpose Scissors
❖ paper towel
❖ water container
❖ fine grit sandpaper

Instructions:

1. Mix six parts Neutral Beige Sandstones medium to one part Country Red acrylic paint.

2. Using the fan paintbrush, apply two generous coats of the mixture all over the shelf, leaving the back of the shelf unfinished. Allow drying time between each coat. Wash the fan paintbrush and blot it dry with paper towel.

3. Use the flat paintbrush to apply two coats of Country Red paint to the back of the shelf, allowing drying time between each coat. Wash the paintbrush and blot it dry with paper towel.

4. Gently sand the surface of the ceramic tiles. Wipe the tiles clean with damp paper towel.

5. With the flat paintbrush, apply an even coat of the Baby Blue paint to each of the tiles, carefully avoiding leaving any brush strokes or streaks. Allow the first coat to dry and apply a second coat. Wash the paintbrush and blot it dry on paper towel.

6. Very carefully place and glue the decoupage motifs on the front surface of each of the three tiles using the UHU glue stick. Be sure not to smear any extra glue on the tiles. Allow the glue to dry completely.

7. Apply a generous coat of tacky glue to the back of each tile. Place each one into the appropriate spot on the shelf. Allow the glue to dry overnight.

8. Spray the shelf, including the tiles, with two to three coats of varnish. Allow drying time between each coat.

9. Mix a small amount of the Baby Blue paint with a large blob of decorating paste. Use your finger to push the coloured paste gently into the grooves between the tiles and the shelf. Do small areas at a time and wipe off any excess with a damp soft cloth. The paste works as a "grout" without scratching the surface of the tiles.

10. Allow the paste to dry overnight. If necessary, apply a second coat of paste to fill the grooves completely.

HINTS, TIPS & GREAT THINGS TO KNOW:

DecoArt Sandstones give a textured finish, so you can apply the product directly onto unsanded objects, which is a great time saver. If sanding isn't your favourite pastime, you're going to love this project (and the other projects in this chapter)! You can use Sandstones in the colours available, or do what I did and add your own colour to a neutral base.

Wastebasket

Materials Required:

- 1 Walnut Hollow medium wastebasket
- DecoArt Americana acrylic paints:
  1 bottle Baby Blue
  1 bottle Marigold
  1 bottle Country Red
- 1 roll narrow KleenEdge painter's tape
- 1 small flat paintbrush
- 2 medium foam paintbrushes
- palette paper
- 1 small sea sponge
- 4 decoupage motifs of your choice
- 1 UHU glue stick
- 1 bottle gloss acrylic varnish
- fine grit sandpaper
- water container
- paper towel
- Fiskars 8" Multi-Purpose Scissors
- hammer
- ruler

Instructions:

1. Thoroughly sand all pieces of the wastebasket and wipe away any particles of dust with damp paper towel.

2. Using the foam paintbrush, apply two coats of the Baby Blue acrylic paint to the fronts and edges of all pieces. Allow drying time between each coat.

3. Repeat step 2 for all sides and edges of the bottom of the wastebasket. Allow paint to dry thoroughly. Wash the paintbrush and blot it dry on paper towel.

4. Paint the reverse side of all pieces with two coats of the Marigold. Allow drying time between each coat.

5. On the Baby Blue side of all pieces, measure approximately 1½ inches (4 cm) in from each edge. Tape off a 1¼-inch (3-cm) border around each side, using the painter's tape.

6. On the palette paper, drizzle first the Country Red paint, then the Baby Blue and last the Marigold, one colour on top of the next. Do not mix the paints.

7. Gently dip the damp sea sponge into the swirls of paint. Blot some of the paint on paper towel. Sponge the paint onto the middle area of each of the wastebasket sides. Allow the paint to dry completely.

8. Tape off another ½-inch (1-cm) border around the sponged area and paint this area with the Country Red, using the small flat paintbrush. Repeat on all sides, using two coats to cover. Remove the tape. Allow this border to dry. Wash the paintbrush and blot it dry with paper towel.

9. Turn all pieces over to the Marigold side. Tape off a ½-inch (1-cm) border around the edges, and paint it with two coats of Country Red, allowing drying time between each coat. Remove the tape. Wash the paintbrush and blot it dry on paper towel.

10. Turn the pieces back to the blue side. Using the glue stick, apply two decoupage motifs on one side of the wastebasket. Match the sides together to ensure you have the proper opposite side, and apply the other two motifs on the opposite side. Allow the glue to dry.

11. Assemble the wastebasket according to the manufacturer's instructions, being careful not to chip the paint when hammering. Place a soft cloth or paper towel between the hammer and the wood when inserting the nails to avoid damage.

12. Apply two to three coats of acrylic varnish on the entire wastebasket, allowing drying time in between each coat. Wash the paintbrush and blot it dry on paper towel.

HINTS, TIPS & GREAT THINGS TO KNOW:

Some of us like to hide our wastebaskets, perhaps under the sink. I prefer to make any wastebaskets I have in the house decorative. Because you want a powder room wastebasket to be functional, you need to apply several coats of varnish covering the paint and decorating, so you can clean it easily. You will notice I have used this wastebasket to hold extra towels.

Wall Accents

Materials Required:

- ❖ 2 plaster wall pieces, 1 large, 1 small
- ❖ DecoArt Sandstones:
  1 jar Neutral Beige
- ❖ DecoArt Americana acrylic paint:
  1 bottle Country Red
- ❖ 1 can gloss acrylic spray varnish
- ❖ 1 fan paintbrush
- ❖ water container
- ❖ paper towel

Instructions:

1. Mix a small amount (no more than 20 percent) of Country Red paint with the entire jar of Neutral Beige Sandstones until it is the desired colour.

2. Using the fan paintbrush, apply a generous coat of the mixture to both wall pieces. Allow the mixture to dry and apply a generous second coat. Allow the mixture to dry thoroughly. Wash the fan paintbrush and blot it dry on paper towel.

3. In a well-ventilated area, spray each item with two to three coats of varnish, allowing drying time between each coat.

4. Hang the wall pieces on the wall in a pleasing arrangement.

HINTS, TIPS & GREAT THINGS TO KNOW:

The more you stir Sandstones, the more liquified the medium becomes. If you find you have stirred it too much and you wish a thicker consistency, simply wait a few minutes and it will thicken up again. This characteristic allows you to apply the product in any manner you wish. These decorative accents were added to this powder room to enhance the look of the room as well as being functional. I have used plaster moons; however, you may choose any wall accents you wish.

Rack-It-Up Towel Holder

Materials Required:

❖ 1 Walnut Hollow 18-inch (46-cm)
  towel holder
❖ DecoArt Americana acrylic paints:
  1 bottle Baby Blue
  1 bottle Country Red
  1 bottle Marigold
❖ 3 decoupage motifs of your choice
❖ 1 medium foam paintbrush
❖ 1 small angular paintbrush
❖ 1 UHU glue stick
❖ 1 bottle gloss acrylic varnish
❖ fine grit sandpaper
❖ water container
❖ paper towel

Instructions:

1. Sand the towel rack thoroughly and wipe away any dust particles with a damp paper towel.

2. Using the medium foam paintbrush, paint the front of the rack, excluding the towel rod and towel rod holders, with two coats of the Baby Blue paint. Allow drying time between each coat. Wash the paintbrush and blot it dry with paper towel.

3. Use the angular brush to paint the edges and towel rod holders with two coats of the Country Red paint. Allow drying time between each coat. Wash the paintbrush and blot it dry on paper towel.

4. Paint the end of each towel rod holder with the Marigold paint. Wash the paintbrush and blot it dry with paper towel.

5. With the angular paintbrush, apply two coats of the Marigold paint to the towel rod. Allow drying time between each coat. Wash the paintbrush and blot it dry with paper towel.

6. Use the glue stick to apply the decoupage motifs to the front of the towel rack. Allow the glue to dry.

7. Apply two to three coats of acrylic varnish to all areas of the towel rack, allowing drying time in between coats. Wash the paintbrush and blot it dry on paper towel.

HINTS, TIPS & GREAT THINGS TO KNOW:

I have decorated this powder room with a playful, celestial theme; however, the choice of theme is yours. Keep in mind that I have coordinated paint colours and decorative items within this room. You may choose to make one or two items and change the colours. Feel free to substitute various wood products and simply incorporate some of the ideas. I have used the same style of decoupage motifs for several of the projects in this room. You may want to do the same, or mix them up a little. The sky's the limit!

Fabric Picture Montage

Materials Required:

- Fredrix Artists Canvas panels:
  1 each 18 x 24 inches (46 cm x 61 cm)
  1 each 16 x 20 inches (41 cm x 50 cm)
  1 each 12 x 16 inches (30 cm x 41 cm)
  3 each 4 x 6 inches (10 cm x 15 cm)
- 1½ yards (1.4 m) decorator fabric
- 1 can Elmer's Spray Adhesive
- 1 bottle Aleene's Designer Tacky Glue
- 2 rolls double-sided mounting tape
- Fiskars Softouch Multi-Purpose Scissors
- paper towel
- ruler

Instructions:

1. Using each canvas as a guide, cut pieces of fabric 1 inch (2.5 cm) larger on all sides for each panel.

2. In a well-ventilated area, spray the adhesive on the front of a canvas panel. Lay the panel face down on the wrong side of the appropriate piece of fabric and press. Turn the panel over and smooth the fabric over the front of the panel.

3. Place the panel right side down and use your finger to apply a small amount of the glue to the exposed fabric. Fold the edges over to the back of the panel, gluing the corners neatly. Allow the glue to dry overnight.

4. Repeat steps 2 and 3 for each of the canvas panels.

5. Arrange the fabric pictures in a pleasing manner on the floor before adhering them to the wall. When you have decided on the pattern, apply a generous amount of the double-sided mounting tape to the backs of the panels and push them firmly in place on the wall.

HINTS, TIPS & GREAT THINGS TO KNOW:

Decorating your walls doesn't have to be an expensive venture. I have used this technique in various rooms in my house. Covering canvas panels with fabric gives a splash of colour to any wall. Be sure to purchase good-quality mounting tape, or investigate the other methods available to adhere decorative items to your walls without any damage.

CHAPTER FIVE

The Master Bedroom

This is my favourite room in the house. I wanted a romantic, soft look in this bedroom, without appearing too feminine. I love a monochromatic colour scheme, with tints, tones and hues of the same base colour. The finished look is fabulous. We use this room a lot for reading and, therefore, I set aside an area for soft, comfortable chairs and a small table. I decided to have some fun with the sheets and pillowcases by using a fleur-de-lis stencil to enhance relatively inexpensive bed linens. I added an exquisite silk flower arrangement with roses as the focal flower, and a dainty privacy screen designed to move around the room, depending on what I want to hide. Once again, recycling comes into play, with gilded old picture frames and, last but certainly not least, the wonderful fresco lamps. Judge the results for yourself.

Fleur-de-Lis Bed Linens

Materials Required:

- 1 set plain light-coloured sheets and pillowcases
- DecoArt Easy Blend stencil paint:
  1 jar Ebony Black
  1 jar Antique Gold
  1 jar Ivory
- 3 long stencil blanks
- 3 small stencil brushes
- 1 fine-tipped permanent black marker
- 1 roll stencil tape
- X-Acto knife
- iron and ironing board
- ruler
- paper towel
- water container
- clothes dryer

Instructions:

1. Wash and dry the bed linens without using fabric softener or dryer sheets. Press everything well, using the steam setting on the iron.

2. Find an image you like. I used a fleur-de-lis design; however, you can use anything you wish. Decide which area of the design will be the background, which area will be the focal colour and which area has the finishing details.

3. Place one of the stencil blanks over the image. Using the black marker, trace the area of the image you want as the background of your design. Set this stencil blank aside.

4. Using the second blank, trace out the overlay area for the focus of your design. Set this stencil blank aside.

5. On the third blank, trace out the detail markings.

6. On a well-protected, hard surface, cut out the images with the X-Acto knife. Mark the stencils #1, #2 and #3, with #1 as the background, #2 the focal area and #3 the detail.

7. Place the top sheet of bed linen right side up on a working table. Use the stencil tape to hold the sheet in place.

8. Along the top edge of the sheet, tape stencil #1 in place where you want the design to appear. Make a note of where the design starts and ends so you can line the rest of the pattern up.

9. Swirl the first stencil brush into the Ivory paint and remove the excess on paper towel. In a circular motion, fill in the open area of the stencil. Lift the stencil and move it to create the next image. Continue along the entire top edge of the sheet. Ensure the space between each image is the same, and wash the stencil as needed to avoid any excess paint rubbing off on other areas of the sheet.

10. Place stencil #2 on top of the images left by stencil #1. Change brushes and use the Antique Gold paint to stencil this area. Continue until you have done the entire sheet.

11. Repeat step 10 using stencil #3 and the Ebony Black paint.

12. Repeat steps 7 to 11 on the edge of the two pillowcases.

13. Allow the paint to dry at least 72 hours. Use the dryer to set the paint by tumbling the linens on low for 30 minutes.

HINTS, TIPS & GREAT THINGS TO KNOW:

Challenge yourself. If you have had a bit of experience using commercially manufactured stencils, you might be ready to create your own. In this case, I used a three-part stencil in an overlay fashion. The three different stencils are all part of one design. By creating an overlay effect, you can achieve a higher end stencilled result.

Recycled Picture Frames

Materials Required:

- ❖ 2 to 3 old wooden picture frames
- ❖ 1 bottle Houston Art Gold Leaf Adhesive Size
- ❖ 1 package Houston Art Gold Leaf
- ❖ DecoArt Americana acrylic paint: 1 bottle Buttermilk
- ❖ 1 bottle matte acrylic varnish
- ❖ 2 small foam paintbrushes
- ❖ fine grit sandpaper
- ❖ paper towel
- ❖ water container

Instructions:

1. Sand the frames well with the fine grit sandpaper. Use a damp paper towel to remove all dust particles.

2. Using one of the small foam paintbrushes, apply two to three coats of the Buttermilk paint to both sides of the frames. Allow drying time between each coat. Wash the paintbrush and blot it dry on paper towel.

3. Using the second small foam paintbrush, apply the gold leaf adhesive to random areas

of the front of the frames; leaving areas free of the adhesive. The gold leaf will adhere only to the adhesive. Allow the adhesive to dry for two hours or until completely clear. Wash the foam paintbrush and blot it dry on paper towel.

4. Apply one sheet of gold leaf at a time to the front of a frame, gently smoothing with a dry paintbrush. Continue until the fronts of each frame have been covered.

5. Continue stroking gently with the paint-brush, so the leaf comes away from the areas where the adhesive was not applied, leaving open areas of the paint colour showing through. Remove all loose leaf.

6. Repeat steps 3 to 5 on the backs of the frames, as portions of this area will show when the frames are hung on the wall.

7. Apply two to three coats of the acrylic varnish to both frames, allowing drying time between each coat. Wash the foam paintbrush and blot it dry on paper towel.

8. Hang the picture frames in a pleasing manner on the wall.

HINTS, TIPS & GREAT THINGS TO KNOW:

Here's a great opportunity to go hunting through garage sales and antique markets for those wonderful finds that can be turned into beautiful home decor projects. Look for frames with good structure, and not too much damage. Bumps and nicks are good as they give the finished project character.

Roses on a Pedestal

Materials Required:

- 1 large round container, approximately 14 inches (35 cm) high
- assortment of Winward Silks flowers:
  7 stems large open Roses
  9 stems Rose Buds
  6 stems Sweetpea
  7 stems Delphinium or Lilac
  5 stems artificial Eucalyptus
- 3 large blocks Sahara floral foam
- newspaper
- 1 small bag Spanish or sheet moss
- 5 yards (4.5 m) Offray sheer 3-inch (8-cm) ribbon
- 1 roll floral stem wrap
- 1 bag floral "U" pins
- floral knife
- 1 paddle 24-26 gauge floral wire
- glue gun and glue sticks
- Fiskars Craft Snips
- Fiskars 8" Multi-Purpose Scissors

Instructions:

1. Fill the bottom of the container with newspaper.

2. Using the floral knife, cut the foam to fit snugly in the opening of the container. Secure the foam in place by applying a small amount of hot glue to the edges of the container.

3. Cover the foam with moss and secure it with the floral "U" pins. Allow some of the moss to drape over the sides of the container.

4. Using the Craft Snips, cut the stem of one rose to approximately 1½ times the height of the container. Glue the rose in the middle of the arrangement. (Keep the discarded stems handy!)

5. Cut two more open roses approximately 6 inches (15 cm) shorter than the first one. Insert and glue these roses to the left and right of the first flower.

6. Cut, insert and glue another open rose so it's long enough to hang 5 to 6 inches (12.5 cm to 15 cm) down the front of the container. Insert and glue the rest of the roses throughout the arrangement, cutting the stems according to where you place them.

7. Insert and glue one stem of sweetpea in the middle of the arrangement, slightly behind the tallest rose. The sweetpea should be slightly taller.

8. Insert and glue another stem of sweetpea so it drapes down the front of the container, under the rose.

9. Cut the remaining sweetpea stems apart, gluing the pieces throughout the arrangement.

10. Cut the stems of all the rose buds to the appropriate length for filling any open areas. Insert and glue them in place.

11. Insert and glue one full stem of eucalyptus in the middle of the arrangement, behind the flowers. Insert and glue another piece so it drapes down the front of the container, behind the flowers.

12. Cut the remaining eucalyptus stems apart and glue them into the design in a pleasing manner. Be sure to put some of the eucalyptus and floral stems at the back of the arrangement; however, remember that this design is viewed from the front so the back of the design should be relatively flat.

13. Insert and glue one stem of delphinium or lilac in the centre of the arrangement, and one to the left and right side of the first stem. Cut three more delphinium stems slightly shorter and glue them in the lower front area. Cut the last stem to fit in any area you detect an opening.

14. Make a multi-loop bow using the sheer ribbon and wire. Attach a piece of discarded stem to the bow by placing the stem against the wired area of the bow. Wind any leftover wire from the bow around the stem. Cover the stem with floral tape, securing the stem to the bow.

15. Insert and glue the bow to the lower right side of the arrangement.

HINTS, TIPS & GREAT THINGS TO KNOW:

This floral design creates an impact. It stands alone on a pedestal and is viewed from the front only. You can choose whatever colour combinations work for you. I have designed mine in cream and gold to enhance the master bedroom, which is decorated in a monochromatic colour scheme. You can either use a pedestal to display the design or place it on a piece of furniture in the room. However you decide to use it, have fun putting it together!

Privacy Screen

Materials Required:

- ❖ 1 Walnut Hollow privacy screen
- ❖ DecoArt Dazzling Metallics:
  2 bottles Glorious Gold
- ❖ DecoArt Americana acrylic paint:
  2 bottles Buttermilk
- ❖ 3 bottles DecoArt Weathered Wood
  crackle medium
- ❖ 3 small foam paintbrushes
- ❖ 1 large sea sponge
- ❖ 1 roll stencil tape
- ❖ 1 large bottle satin acrylic varnish
- ❖ sheer fabric for panels as specified
  for the privacy screen
- ❖ sewing machine
- ❖ thread
- ❖ Fiskars 9½" Bent Shears
- ❖ water container
- ❖ paper towel
- ❖ fine grit sandpaper
- ❖ carpenter's glue
- ❖ palette paper
- ❖ ruler
- ❖ pencil

Instructions

1. Remove all the pieces from the box. Read all directions carefully before beginning. Check for all pieces and know what everything is used for.

2. Sand all pieces well with the fine grit sandpaper. Remove all dust particles with damp paper towel.

3. Using one of the small foam paintbrushes, apply a coat of the Glorious Gold Metallic paint to all sides of all the wood pieces. Allow the paint to dry.

4. Gently sand all pieces again and remove dust particles with damp paper towel. Apply a second coat of gold paint, and allow it to dry. Repeat the sanding process. Set the dowel pieces aside. Wash the paintbrush and blot it dry on paper towel.

5. Use the stencil tape to mask off the edges of all pieces. You will apply the crackle medium to the flat areas of the wood only.

6. Follow the directions on the crackle medium packaging to apply an even coat of crackle to one side of all pieces, using a clean brush. Allow the crackle to dry completely, at least 2 hours. Wash the paintbrush and blot it dry on paper towel.

7. Dampen the sea sponge and remove any excess water with paper towel. Squeeze a generous amount of the Buttermilk paint onto a piece of palette paper. Dip the sea sponge into the paint and apply the paint generously over the crackle medium, covering it completely. Be sure to apply an even coat and do not go over areas where you have already applied the paint. The crackle medium will dry and crack the paint immediately. Continue this process for all pieces of wood. Allow the paint to dry completely.

8. Turn all pieces over and repeat steps 6 and 7 for the other side of each piece. Allow the paint to dry thoroughly.

9. Use a foam paintbrush to apply two coats of varnish to all pieces. Allow drying time between each coat.

10. Assemble the screen according to the manufacturer's instructions.

11. Sew fabric panels for the screen according to the manufacturer's instructions.

HINTS, TIPS & GREAT THINGS TO KNOW:

This privacy screen arrives unassembled, which allows you to use whatever paint or stain technique you want before putting it together. You need a large working area, as the pieces are quite large. The crackle effect creates a wonderful, old-world look. I have mixed that look with a trendy sheer fabric with an animal print for the panels, to add some interest. The instructions for assembling the screen and making the panels are included in the packaging.

Fresco Lamps

Materials Required:

- 2 ceramic lamp bases, lamp shades removed
- DecoArt Americana acrylic paint: 1 bottle Buttermilk
- 1 jar Liquitex Gloss Heavy Gel Medium
- 1 fan paintbrush
- 1 small foam paintbrush
- medium grit sandpaper
- water container
- paper towel

HINTS, TIPS & GREAT THINGS TO KNOW:

Everything old is new again! My basement has housed two old-style ceramic lamps for what seems like forever. I think the reason I kept them around was because I liked their shape. This project allowed me to take those older lamp bases and recycle them. Because I didn't spend any money on the lamps themselves, I was able to treat myself to two new lampshades, plus add a touch of sophistication with these two wonderful finials.

Instructions:

1. Sand the lamp bases down to remove any gloss from the existing glaze. Wipe the lamps well with a damp paper towel.

2. With the foam paintbrush, apply a thin coat of the Buttermilk paint to the surface of the lamp bases. Allow the first coat to dry and apply a second coat. Allow the paint to dry thoroughly. Wash the paintbrush and blot it dry on paper towel.

3. Mix the jar of gel medium well with approximately 1 ounce (28 g) of the Buttermilk paint.

4. Using the fan paintbrush, apply a thin coat of gel medium over the surface of the lamp bases, swirling the medium as you apply it. Allow the first coat to dry overnight. Wash the fanbrush and blot it dry on paper towel.

5. In the same manner as step 4, apply a second and third coat, allowing each coat to dry in between. Create a swirl pattern each time you apply a coat. Allow each coast to dry thoroughly overnight. Wash the fanbrush and blot it dry on paper towel

6. Attach lamp shades and decorative finials.

CHAPTER SIX

The Children's Bedroom

Time really does fly, and before you know it, the kids are racing through school and headlong into their teens. I wanted to create a look for my son that he would enjoy for several years. The idea was to keep the decorating simple, as well as easy to maintain. I started with denim, and before I knew it, I had developed a theme. I incorporated a second checked fabric, which draws several other colours into the room. A few bandanas, a bit of suede lacing, a concho here and there, and I had a great look with little time or expense. You can choose from a wonderful assortment of projects for your look, changing the fabrics and colours to suit your own decor. The great thing about denim is it works for both boys and girls. This chapter hosts creative projects—a decoupaged clock, a denim-look waste bin, pillows, a laundry bag and picture frames—to make this room a cozy and functional place for your kids to spend their time. My son loves it, and that's the important part!

Western Clock

Materials Required:

- 1 Walnut Hollow 9- x 12-inch (23-cm x 30-cm) Early American Clock with 3-inch (8-cm) Arabic Bezel
- DecoArt Americana acrylic paint: 1 bottle Burnt Sienna
- 1 bottle satin acrylic varnish
- 1 large UHU glue stick
- wrapping paper, photos, magazine pictures of your choice
- 1 large silver concho

- ¼ yard (0.2 m) brown suede lacing
- several assorted beads
- 1 small foam paintbrush
- 1 1-inch (2.5 cm) flat paintbrush
- glue gun and glue sticks
- Fiskars 8" Multi-Purpose Scissors
- fine grit sandpaper
- paper towel
- water container

Instructions:

1. Remove the clock movement and set aside. Sand the clock well and remove any dust particles with a damp paper towel.

2. Use the foam paintbrush to apply one coat of the acrylic varnish to the clock to seal the wood. Allow drying time. Wash the brush and blot it dry with paper towel.

3. With the foam paintbrush, apply two to three coats of the Burnt Sienna paint to the edges and back of the clock. Allow drying time and sand gently between coats. Wash the brush and blot it dry on paper towel.

4. Cut the wrapping paper in medium-sized pieces. Using the glue stick, apply the paper over the top surface of the clock, covering the wood completely.

5. Trim any excess pieces overlapping the edges with scissors.

6. If you like, remove the outside metal rim from the clock movement. Cut small strips of the paper and wrap them around the metal rim, covering it completely. Use the glue gun to glue the ends in place. Replace the covered metal rim on the clock movement.

7. Using the fine grit sandpaper, distress the wooden edges of the clock by gently sanding away the paint in random areas. Wipe all dust particles with a damp paper towel.

8. With the large flat paintbrush, apply the varnish to the top portion of the clock. Apply five coats, allowing each to dry thoroughly. Sand gently and remove any dust particles. Apply 20 to 30 coats of varnish, sanding every five coats until the clock is completely smooth.

9. Apply two coats of varnish to the edges and back of the clock, allowing drying time between each coat. Wash the paintbrush and blot it dry on paper towel

10. Insert the clock movement.

11. Attach a small piece of suede lacing to the concho, leaving 4-inch (10-cm) tails. Apply several beads to each tail and knot the ends of the lacing.

12. Use the glue gun to glue the concho in place just below the clock movement.

HINTS, TIPS & GREAT THINGS TO KNOW:

My son's room is decorated with a Navaho/Western feel, so I have chosen a very western-looking wrapping paper for this project. Simply choose the paper or photos that work with your decorating scheme, and follow the instructions I give here. Of course, you will probably want to change the paint colour to coordinate, and the concho may become buttons or jewels for a girl.

Denim-Look Waste Bin

Materials Required:

- 1 large wooden waste bin
- 1 can Krylon All-Purpose White spray primer
- 1 can matte acrylic spray varnish
- DecoArt Americana acrylic paints:
  1 bottle White
  1 bottle Admiral Blue
- 1 bottle DecoArt Faux Glazing Medium
- 1 Plaid Weaver brush
- 1 red bandanna
- 1 large metal concho
- ½ yard (0.5 m) brown suede lacing
- several beads
- 1 large foam paintbrush
- 1 small flat paintbrush
- 1 roll KleenEdge painter's tape
- staple gun and staples
- glue gun and glue sticks
- Fiskars 8" Multi-Purpose Scissors
- fine grit sandpaper
- water container
- paper towel

Instructions:

1. Sand the wooden bin completely. Use a damp paper towel to remove any dust particles.

2. In a well-ventilated area, spray the inside and out of the bin with the white spray primer. Allow the primer to dry thoroughly.

3. Apply two coats of the White paint to the inside and out using the large foam paintbrush. Allow drying time between each coat. Wash the brush and blot it dry on paper towel.

4. Mix two parts Admiral Blue paint to four parts Faux Glazing Medium. Using the large foam paintbrush, apply a coat of the blue glaze evenly to one side of the bin, painting over the white paint. With the weaver brush, start at the top of the wooden bin and draw the brush evenly across the glaze in a vertical line. Repeat all the way down the side of the bin. Remove any excess glaze from the brush as you go.

5. Draw the weaver brush across the same side, this time horizontally to create a woven look.

6. Repeat steps 4 and 5 on the other sides of the bin, leaving the inside white. Allow the glaze to dry thoroughly. Wash the weaver brush and blot it dry on paper towel.

7. Using the painter's tape, mask off a ¼-inch (6-mm) border on each side of the bin. Paint two coats of White paint on the border with the small flat paintbrush. Allow drying time between each coat. Wash the paintbrush and blot it dry on paper towel.

8. Apply two to three coats of spray varnish to all areas of the bin and allow drying time between each coat.

9. Arrange the bandanna like a kerchief on one side of the bin. Staple it several times in various areas to hold it in place.

10. Insert the suede lacing into the concho. Add beads to the tails and knot the ends to hold the beads in place. Glue the concho to the centre of the bandana.

HINTS, TIPS & GREAT THINGS TO KNOW:

Another great idea is to use the wallpaper used in the room to accessorize smaller items, such as wastebaskets and desk accessories. Borders work especially well, as the pattern on a border is usually somewhat smaller and more adaptable. I like to use a glue stick, but diluted white glue or podge work, too.

HINTS, TIPS & GREAT THINGS TO KNOW:

The instructions here are for a large bolster-style pillow, which kids can rest their heads on while reading or watching television. There are many great pillow styles you can use in your kids' room. I love to flip through the pattern books in my local fabric shop to get lots of great ideas for new styles. These instructions are easy to follow without a pattern. Your kids will love it!

Bolster Pillow

Materials Required:

- 1 bolster pillow insert (approximately 24 inches/61 cm in length x 24 inches/61 cm in diameter)
- 1½ yards (1.4 m) 60-inch (150-cm) wide denim fabric
- 1 red bandanna
- 1 package light brown suede lacing
- 1 silver concho
- several assorted beads
- Fiskars Softouch Multi-Purpose Scissors
- red thread
- straight pins
- sewing machine
- measuring tape
- fabric glue
- iron and ironing board

Instructions:

1. Wash and dry the denim fabric and bandanna without using fabric softener or dryer sheets. Press everything flat.

2. Cut one main piece of denim 28 x 28 inches (71 cm x 71 cm). Cut two side pieces 28 x 10 inches (71 cm x 25 cm) each.

3. Lay the bandanna flat, right side up, on the right side of the main piece of denim. Pin it in place.

4. Using a zig zag stitch on the sewing machine, overstitch the bandanna to the denim. Press everything flat.

5. Place the long edge of one side piece to one long edge of the main piece of denim, right sides together. Leaving a ¼-inch (0.5-cm) seam allowance, stitch the pieces together using a straight stitch. Repeat on the other side. Press all seams flat towards the main piece of denim.

6. Topstitch the two side seams using the red thread and keeping the stitching ¼ inch (0.5 cm) parallel to the seam. Press seams flat.

7. With rights sides together, pin the two long sides of the denim pillow covering together, leaving a 1½-inch (4-cm) seam allowance. Stitch the seam, using a straight stitch. Trim and press the seam flat.

8. Stitch a double ¼-inch (0.5-cm) hem on each of the two open ends of the pillow. Press the hems flat.

9. Insert the pillow form inside the denim pillow covering so it's in the centre.

10. Cut six 36-inch (91-cm) strands of suede lacing. Separate the strands into two groups of three. With one group, tie a knot 4 inches (10 cm) from one end. Braid the lacing (taping the knot end to a table makes this easier!). Continue to braid, until there is a 4-inch (10-cm) tail at the other end. Tie a knot. Thread three to four beads on each strand and knot each end. Repeat with the other group of lacing.

11. Tie one braid around each end of the pillow.

12. Insert an 8-inch (20-cm) piece of suede lacing and several beads to the concho and glue the concho in the middle of the bandanna.

Cowboy Boot Picture Frame

Materials Required:

- 1 Walnut Hollow wooden picture frame with wide sides
- DecoArt Americana acrylic paints:
  1 bottle White
  1 bottle Admiral Blue
  1 bottle Raw Sienna
- 1 bottle DecoArt Faux Glazing Medium
- 1 "western" stencil
- 1 Plaid Weaver brush
- 1 bottle matte acrylic varnish

- 1 1-inch (2.5-cm) flat paintbrush
- 1 small stencil brush
- 1 small foam paintbrush
- 1 fine-tipped black permanent marker
- 1 roll stencil tape
- fine grit sandpaper
- paper towel
- water container
- ruler
- pencil

96

Instructions:

1. Sand the picture frame well, and wipe away all dust particles with a damp paper towel.

2. Using the flat paintbrush, apply two coats of White paint to all sides of the frame. Allow drying time between each coat. Wash the brush and blot it dry on paper towel.

3. Measure approximately ⅔ of the way from the left side of the frame towards the middle opening. Apply a piece of stencil tape from the top of the frame to the bottom to divide this area from the rest of the frame.

4. Mix two parts Admiral Blue paint with four parts Faux Glazing Medium.

5. With the small foam paintbrush, apply a coat of the blue glaze to the right side of the front and edges of the frame. Run the weaver brush through the glaze vertically. Wipe any excess glaze from the brush. Repeat, running the brush horizontally for a woven denim-fabric look. Allow the glaze to dry and remove the tape. Wash the brushes and blot them dry on paper towel.

6. To stencil the western image onto the frame, tape the stencil at the top of the white portion of the frame. Dip the stencil brush into the Raw Sienna paint and blot most of the paint off the brush. Begin pouncing up and down on the stencil until you have filled the image in. Remove the stencil. Repeat this process two more times down the white area of the frame. Allow the paint to dry thoroughly. Wash and blot the stencil brush dry on paper towel.

7. Once the images are dry, use the permanent marker to make any decorative markings on the image.

8. Using the small foam paintbrush, apply two to three coats of the varnish to the frame, allowing drying time in between coats. Wash the paintbrush and blot it dry on paper towel.

HINTS, TIPS & GREAT THINGS TO KNOW:

If you're really into stencilling, there are many ways to create your own unique effects on your projects. You don't necessarily have to purchase a commercial stencil—you can easily make your own. Try using heavy cardboard, which gives a clean, clear image. This way, you have the opportunity to play around with ideas to get the exact look you want.

Lasso Laundry Bag

Materials Required:

- ❖ 2 yards (1.8 m) 60-inch (150-cm) wide denim fabric
- ❖ 1 red bandanna
- ❖ 10 large grommets with grommet tool
- ❖ 5 small screw hooks
- ❖ sewing machine
- ❖ Fiskars Softouch Multi-Purpose Scissors
- ❖ straight pins
- ❖ measuring tape
- ❖ pencil
- ❖ iron and ironing board

Instructions:

1. Wash and dry the denim fabric and bandanna without using fabric softener or dryer sheets. Press everything flat.

2. Cut two pieces of denim 41 x 30 inches (104 cm x 76 cm) each. Cut one piece of denim 30 x 30 inches (76 cm x 76 cm). The two large pieces form the bag and the small piece forms a pocket on the outside front of the bag.

3. On the small piece of denim, turn under a ¼-inch (0.5-cm) hem at the top and press. Then turn under and pin a 1½-inch (4-cm) hem and press. Using the red thread, topstitch the hem in place and press flat.

4. Cut the bandanna in half. Pin the long edge of the bandanna, right side up, along the topstitching on the right side of the small piece of denim. Topstitch the bandanna to the denim using the zigzag setting on the sewing machine. Press flat.

5. Pin the wrong side of the small piece of denim to the right side of one large piece of denim, matching the bottom raw edges. Sew the side seams, leaving a ¼-inch (0.5-cm) seam allowance. This forms an outside pocket on the bag.

6. Measure to find the centre of the pocket. Topstitch two rows ¼-inch (0.5-cm) apart down the centre to divide the pocket in half. Press flat.

7. Pin the two large pieces of denim with rights sides together, matching the sides evenly. Sew a ¼-inch (0.5-cm) seam allowance on both sides of the bag. Finish seams with a zigzag stitch.

8. To create a flat bottom for the bag, cut a 3- x 3-inch (8-cm x 8-cm) square from both bottom corners of the bag. Open up one corner and match the long edges. Sew a ¼-inch (0.5-cm) seam allowance and press flat. Repeat with the other corner.

9. Turn the bag right side out. Turn under a ¼-inch (0.5-cm) hem on the top edge of the bag. Press flat. Turn under another 4 inches (10 cm). Press and pin in place. Topstitch two rows ¼-inch (0.5-cm) apart to secure the hem. Press.

10. Measure 2 inches (5 cm) from the top edge of the bag and mark the placement of 5 to 6 grommets at equal intervals across the front of the bag. Insert the grommets, following the manufacturer's directions. Lay the bag flat and use a pencil to mark the same grommet placement on the back of the bag. Insert the grommets.

11. Measure and insert five small hooks into the wall, matching the spacing with the grommet placement on the bag. Make sure the bottom of the bag will rest on the floor to avoid straining the hooks.

HINTS, TIPS & GREAT THINGS TO KNOW:

Here's a trick to keep both your kids' clothes and the laundry bag off the floor. Simply hook the bag by the grommets onto the hooks on the wall. When the bag is full, the kids can remove it from the wall and take it to the laundry room to be emptied. Or use the bag as a carryall: weave cording through the grommets and tie.

CHAPTER SEVEN

The Bathroom

I love the animal motifs that are so popular in decorating. There is something mysterious about this look that catches my attention every time I come across it, whether it's in a bed-and-bath shop or in a fabric boutique. It inspires me. I felt decorating a bathroom using an animal print theme would be beautiful, and I was right. In this room, I chose to go a little "wild" and create several projects that would be functional and decorative at the same time. Trimming bath and guest towels with wonderful fabric helps keep costs down, and adding a stencilled planter adds that splash of colour sometimes lacking in a room. Upholster a picture frame, or turn ordinary kitchen canisters into inspiring works of art. A facecloth rack with a fabulous brass elephant finishes this extraordinary look.

Framed Zebra

Materials Required:

- Walnut Hollow large rectangular wooden picture frame
- DecoArt Americana Dazzling Metallics: 1 bottle Glorious Gold
- ½ yard (0.5 m) plain black decorator fabric
- ½ yard (0.5 m) contrasting animal print fabric
- 1 small bag quilt batting
- 2 yards (1.8 m) Domcord Belding thick black cord with a lip
- 2 yards (1.8 m) Domcord Belding flat black trim
- 1 small piece heavy cardboard to fit inside the frame opening
- zebra stamp of your choice
- 1 black ink stamp pad
- 1 small foam paintbrush
- staple gun and staples
- glue gun and glue sticks
- pencil
- Fiskars Softouch Multi-Purpose Scissors
- Fiskars Craft Snips
- 24 to 26 gauge floral wire
- paper towel
- water container
- measuring tape

Instructions:

1. Measure the outside dimensions of the front of the frame. Cut a piece of quilt batting the size of the front of the frame, less approximately ¼ inch (6 mm). Using a small amount of glue, adhere the batting to the front of the frame. Cut away the batting covering the frame opening.

2. Measure and cut a piece of the black fabric approximately 3 inches (8 cm) larger on all sides than the size of the front of the frame.

3. Place the fabric over the batting right side up, with all edges even. Flip the frame over and wrap the excess fabric edges to the back of the frame. Use the staple gun to staple the fabric to the back of the frame, working from side to side and pulling the fabric taut as you go. Staple the corners for a smooth finish.

4. Cut a slit in the middle of the fabric covering the frame opening. Cut four small slits into the corners, being careful not to cut in too far.

5. Pull the flaps of material to the back of the frame through the opening. Glue the fabric to the inside of the frame opening, trimming the edges.

6. Cut four small pieces of the contrasting decorator fabric 10 inches (25 cm) in length and 4 inches (10 cm) in width.

7. Glue the end of one of the pieces of fabric inside one side of the opening of the frame, right side up, turning under any raw edges of the fabric. Draw the fabric across the frame and over the side edge to the back, gathering the material slightly as you take it to the back of the frame. Staple the fabric to the back of the frame. Repeat this process for the other three sides of the frame.

8. Measure the opening of the frame and cut a piece of heavy cardboard to fit inside this opening. Using the small foam paintbrush, paint the cardboard with two coats of Glorious Gold paint, allowing drying time between coats. Wash the paintbrush and blot it dry on paper towel.

9. Press the zebra stamp into the inkpad and onto the middle of the piece of painted cardboard. Set the cardboard aside to dry.

10. Glue the cording around the outside edge of the frame, finishing off the ends of the cord with a small amount of glue.

11. Glue the trim on the edges of the frame to cover the lip of the cording.

12. Insert and glue the picture of the zebra into the opening of the frame.

13. Trim off any extra pieces of fabric on the back of the frame. Cut a piece of black fabric 1 inch (2.5 cm) larger on all sides than the frame. Turn the edges under and staple the fabric to the back of the frame every ½ inch (1 cm) to cover all the raw edges of material and cardboard insert.

14. Use the wire and staple gun to create a hanger for the picture.

HINTS, TIPS & GREAT THINGS TO KNOW:

Upholstering can be rather intimidating, especially if you begin with a large project. Using upholstery methods to cover smaller items like a picture frame or small ottoman can give you the confidence to try larger projects. This picture frame is the perfect place to start, and adds elegance and flair to this vibrant bathroom.

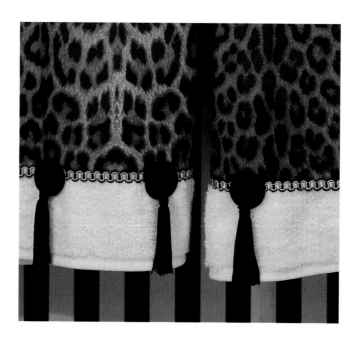

Animal-Themed Guest Towels

Materials Required:

- ❖ 2 large neutral-coloured bath towels
- ❖ 2 small neutral-coloured hand towels
- ❖ 1 yard (1 m) washable animal print fabric or fabric of your choice
- ❖ 6 large medallion tassels
- ❖ 2 small medallion tassels
- ❖ 3 yards (2.75 m) Domcord Belding flat trim
- ❖ 1 small bottle fabric glue
- ❖ thread
- ❖ sewing machine
- ❖ measuring tape
- ❖ straight pins
- ❖ Fiskars Softouch Multi-Purpose Scissors
- ❖ iron and ironing board

Instructions:

1. Wash and dry all fabric and towels, without using fabric softener or dryer sheets. If necessary, press the fabric after washing.

2. Measure the width of the bath towel and add 1 inch (2.5cm). Cut two pieces of fabric using that amount as the length and 11½ inches (29 cm) wide. For example, my bath towels are 29½ inches (75 cm) wide, so I cut my fabric 30½ x 11½ inches (77.5 cm x 29 cm).

3. Turn under ½ inch (1 cm) on all four edges of the fabric piece and press flat. The fabric piece should measure the width of the towel by 10½ inches (27 cm). Pin it to one end of the towel, with the right sides of the fabric piece and the towel facing up, so that 2½ inches (6 cm) of towel shows at the bottom edge.

4. Sew the fabric piece to the towel, keeping everything flat and even as you go.

5. Repeat steps 3 and 4 with the second bath towel.

6. Follow steps 2 to 4 for the small hand towels, measuring 5½ inches (14 cm) (instead of 11½ inches/29cm). The finished piece of fabric should measure 4½ inches (11.5 cm) by the width of your towel.

7. Sew a strip of trim along the upper edge of the fabric inlay on all towels, covering the stitching line. Repeat on the bottom edge of the fabric.

8. Use the fabric glue to apply the large medallion tassels to the bottom edge of the trim on the bath towels according to the manufacturer's directions, overlapping the tassels onto the towel slightly. Measure to ensure the medallions are placed appropriately and visible when you hang your towels. Repeat with the small medallions on the hand towels.

HINTS, TIPS & GREAT THINGS TO KNOW:

Fewer decorative items can be more attractive than many. If you feel three tassels are too much for your size of towel, try using two. When choosing bathroom accents, such as shower curtains, keep the colour soft and prints to a minimum. It's easy to get carried away with too many animal prints.

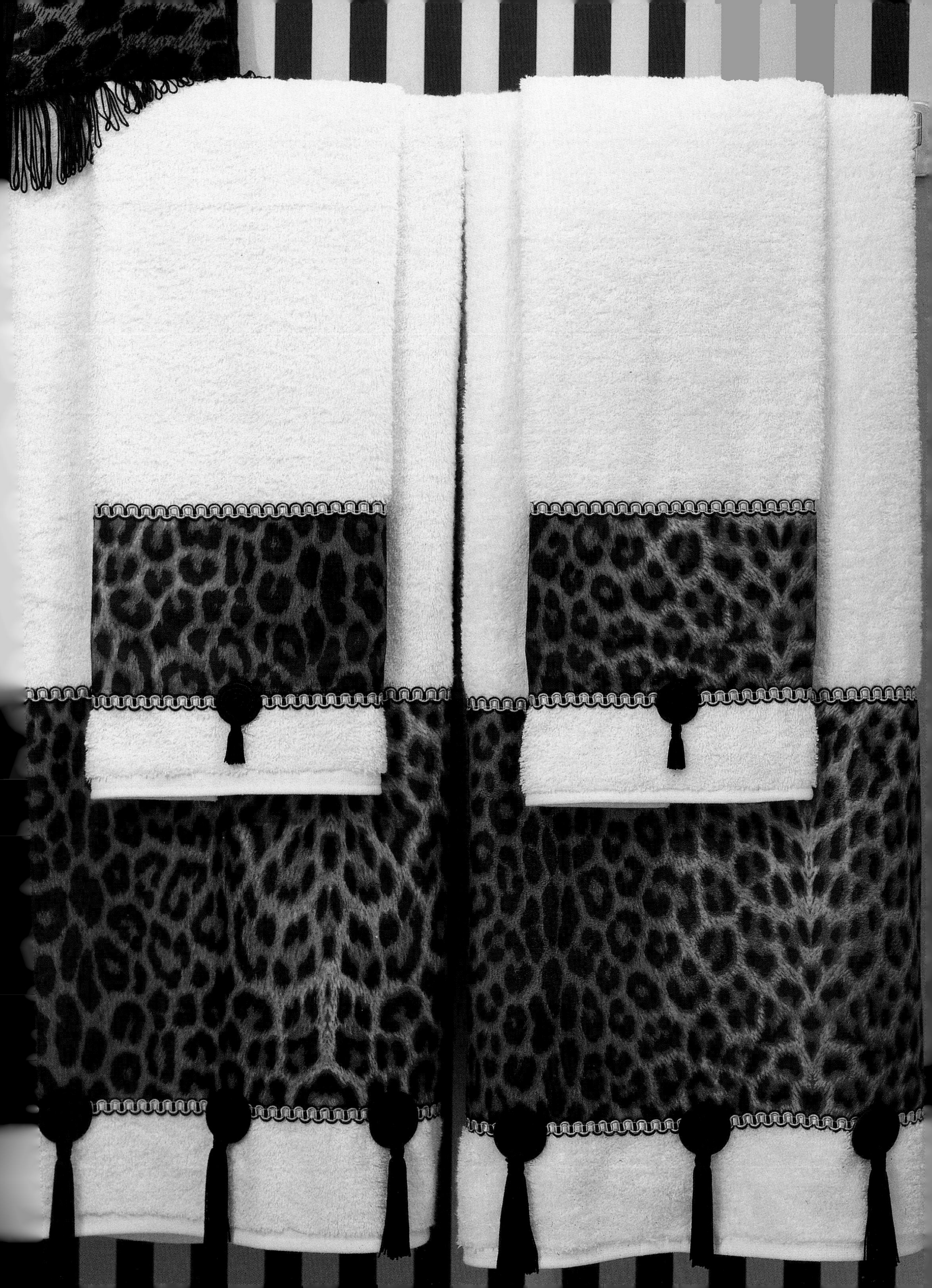

Facecloth Rack

Materials Required:

- Walnut Hollow 11- x 14-inch (28-cm x 35-cm) or 12- x 16-inch (30-cm x 41-cm) wooden oval plaque
- 1 large decorative brass towel fixture
- DecoArt Americana acrylic paints:
  1 bottle Lamp Ebony Black
  1 bottle Buttermilk
- DecoArt Americana Dazzling Metallics:
  1 bottle Glorious Gold
- 1 bottle DecoArt Weathered Wood crackle medium
- 1 small sea sponge
- 1 medium foam paintbrush
- 1 1-inch (2.5-cm) flat paintbrush
- 1 old, small paintbrush
- 1 bottle matte acrylic varnish
- 1 small tube Burnt Umber oil paint
- 1 small tin linseed oil
- 1½ yards (1.4 m) Domcord Belding narrow black cord trim
- fine grit sandpaper
- water container
- paper towel
- soft cloths
- glue gun and glue sticks
- screwdriver
- screws or double-sided mounting tape

Instructions:

1. Sand the plaque well and remove all dust particles with a damp paper towel.

2. Using the foam paintbrush, apply two coats of Lamp Ebony Black paint to the plaque, front and back. Allow drying time between coats. Wash the brush and blot it dry with paper towel.

3. With the flat paintbrush, apply a very thick coat of the crackle medium to the top front of the plaque only. Do not apply the crackle to the edges or back. Make sure the surface is covered well, leaving no dull spots or holes. Allow the crackle to dry 1 to 2 hours. Wash the paintbrush and blot it dry with paper towel.

4. Using a damp sea sponge, apply a heavy coat of the Buttermilk paint over the crackle medium, following the directions on the bottle carefully. Do not go back over previously applied paint. Allow the paint to dry and crack. Wash the sea sponge and blot it dry on paper towel.

5. Use the flat paintbrush to apply two coats of Glorious Gold paint on the edges of the plaque, allowing drying time between coats. Wash the paintbrush and blot it dry on paper towel.

6. Use a soft cloth to apply a thin layer of the linseed oil over the entire front of the plaque. Immediately apply a thin coat of Burnt Umber oil paint in the same manner. While the oil paint is fresh, wipe the excess off with a clean

soft cloth. This process ages the cracks and gives the project the appearance of an antique. Allow it to dry overnight.

7. Apply two to three coats of varnish with the flat paintbrush, allowing drying time between each coat.

8. Using small amounts of hot glue applied with an old paintbrush, attach the cording around the grooved edge of the plaque. Use the screwdriver to attach the brass towel holder to the middle of the plaque.

9. Attach the plaque to the wall with screws or double-sided mounting tape.

HINTS, TIPS & GREAT THINGS TO KNOW:

There are two ways of hanging this plaque. You can drill holes through the plaque and screw it to the wall, or you can use an ample amount of good-quality double-sided mounting tape, which is what I did. Facecloths decorated in the same fabric as the towels accompany the plaque and make a useful addition to any bathroom.

Jungle Jim Planter

Materials Required:

- 1 Walnut Hollow home accessory planter 7.5 x 7.5 x 8.75 inches (19 cm x 19 cm x 22 cm)
- DecoArt Americana acrylic paints:
  1 bottle Lamp Ebony Black
  1 bottle Camel
- DecoArt Easy Blend stencil paints:
  1 bottle Ebony Black
  1 bottle Antique Gold
  1 bottle Forest Green
  1 bottle Yellow Green
  1 bottle Cadmium Yellow
  1 bottle Burnt Sienna
  1 bottle Neutral Grey
- Plaid Decorator Edge Safari Friends Stencil
- 1 roll stencil tape
- 2 to 3 small foam paintbrushes
- 2 to 3 small stencil brushes
- 1 small tin linseed oil
- 1 small tube Burnt Umber oil paint
- fine grit sandpaper
- 1 can matte acrylic spray varnish
- several soft cloths
- paper towel
- water container

Instructions:

1. Sand all pieces of the planter and wipe the pieces clean of any dust particles with damp paper towel.

2. Using a small foam paintbrush, apply two coats of Lamp Ebony Black paint to both sides of the bottom piece of the planter and the wooden feet, allowing drying time between each coat.

3. Paint the other four pieces with two coats of black on one side and Camel on the other, allowing drying time between coats. Paint the edges of these four pieces Camel. Wash all paintbrushes and blot them dry on paper towel.

4. Check the assembly directions frequently to ensure you are working in the right areas on the Camel-painted sides. Choose your designs from one stencil to create a small "jungle scene" on each side of the planter.

5. Tape the stencil in position to avoid any slipping. Load the stencil brush with the first colour of paint, removing the excess onto paper towel. Use the grey stencil paint for the elephant, the black for the zebra, the gold for the giraffe shaded with the brown, the various greens for the tree branches and the various earth tones for the tree trunks. Apply the paint to the design in a circular motion from the outside of the stencil into the middle. To shade, load a second stencil brush with the shading colour (usually a darker shade), again removing some of the paint onto paper towel.

Stencil around the outside edges of the area you wish shaded. Allow the paint to dry overnight. Wash all stencil brushes and blot them dry on paper towel.

6. Use a small foam paintbrush to apply a coat of the linseed oil on top of the design, working with one side at a time. Using a soft cloth, gently rub a thin coat of Burnt Umber oil paint over the linseed oil.

7. Using a clean soft cloth, wipe the excess oil paint off the surface of your design. Allow the oil to dry overnight.

8. Spray all the pieces of the planter, including the bottom and the legs, with two to three coats of varnish, allowing drying time between each coat.

9. Follow the manufacturer's instructions to assemble the planter.

HINTS, TIPS & GREAT THINGS TO KNOW:

Perhaps a planter is not something you would readily think to put in your bathroom. Actually, plants do very well in this environment. Every time you take a shower or bath, the plants get a free steambath, and therefore remain very healthy. If you've got the room, add a plant or two to your bathroom.

Bathroom Canisters

Materials Required:

- ❖ 1 set of 4 glass canisters, preferably with flat sides
- ❖ DecoArt Ultra Gloss Acrylic Enamels:
  1 bottle Gloss Black
  1 bottle Sable Brown
  1 bottle Metallic Bronze
- ❖ 3 Domcord Belding black corded tassels

- ❖ 1 decorative black trim piece
- ❖ 3 soft round paintbrushes
- ❖ glue gun and glue sticks
- ❖ water container
- ❖ paper towel
- ❖ glass cleaner

Instructions:

1. Clean the glass canisters with a glass cleaner before starting. Make sure the glass is free of lint and grease.

2. Shake the paints well and open all three in order to work with them at the same time.

3. Protect your work area and lay all canisters on their sides. This way you are working on a flat surface to prevent the paint from running.

4. Using one paintbrush for each colour, paint one side of the canisters. Make thick squiggly lines with each of the three colours, to form a random pattern. Wash the brushes and blot dry on paper towel.

5. Allow this first side of the canisters to dry overnight and repeat the same process with the rest of the sides and the lids. Allow each side to dry overnight before moving on to the next side.

6. Once you have painted all sides and the lid of each canister, allow all paint to dry and cure for approximately 2 weeks.

7. Place the canisters in a cold oven, making sure they do not touch each other. Heat the oven to 325°F (160°C) and bake for 30 minutes. Let the oven cool down before taking the glass out.

8. Allow the canisters to cool for at least 24 hours before using. Wrap and tie a corded tassel around the neck of each of the larger canisters and glue a decorative trim piece to the small canister.

HINTS, TIPS & GREAT THINGS TO KNOW:

Glass or ceramic canisters are not just for the kitchen. They can be functional pieces in many areas of the house. I like the fact that canisters are larger than most decorative items specifically designed to hold toiletries, so you can fill them up and not worry about replenishing the day-to-day items you need for quite some time. It's fun decorating them to coordinate with your decor.

CHAPTER EIGHT

The Great Outdoors

Sometimes we get so caught up in decorating the inside of our homes, we tend to neglect to work on projects for our patios and decks. I think I may have some simple solutions that will help you make the summer months and all year round full of colour and fun. Start with wonderful coordinating clay pots for those plants and flowers that have spent far too much time trapped in plastic containers. Add the perfect lighting and a fabulous summer centrepiece and you are off to a great start. Just for fun, create a set of durable yet funky place mats that won't mind being forgotten during an occasional soft summer rain. Be sure to enjoy your colourful, summer playground surrounded by friends and family.

Pots, Pots and More Pots

Materials Required:

- several clay pots in various sizes, shapes and designs
- DecoArt Patio Paints:
  - 1 bottle Fern Green
  - 1 bottle Foxglove Pink
  - 1 bottle Sunflower Yellow
  - 1 bottle Deep Waterfall Blue
- DecoArt Heavenly Hues:
  - 1 bottle White Cloud
- 1 small flower stencil of your choice

- 1 roll stencil tape
- 1 medium bottle Plaid Mod Podge gloss
- 1 small package compressed sponge
- 1 small foam spouncer
- 1 small foam paintbrush
- soft cloths
- water container
- paper towel
- Fiskars 8" Multi-Purpose Scissors
- measuring tape

Checkerboard Rimmed Pot

Instructions:

1. Using the foam paintbrush, paint the outside and bottom of the first pot with two to three coats of Fern Green paint. Allow drying time between each coat. Wash the brush and blot it dry with paper towel.

2. Measure the brim of the pot. Cut a square piece of compressed sponge using half that amount. For example, if the brim measures 2 inches (5 cm), cut a 1- x 1-inch (2.5-cm x 2.5-cm) square. Cut several squares and place them in water so they expand. Squeeze them dry with paper towel.

3. Dip one of the sponge squares into Foxglove Pink paint. Then tip one side of the square into Sunflower Yellow paint.

4. Sponge a checkerboard pattern around the rim of the pot, reloading the sponge as you go. Allow the paint to dry thoroughly.

5. Use the foam paintbrush to apply a coat of the Mod Podge on the inside of the pot to protect it. Allow to dry. Wash the brush thoroughly and blot it dry with paper towel.

White-Washed Pot

Instructions:

1. Choose a pot with dimension for the most effective results.

2. Use the small foam paintbrush to apply two to three coats of Deep Waterfall Blue paint to the outside and bottom of the pot. Allow drying time between each coat. Wash the brush and blot it dry with paper towel.

3. Apply a coat of White Cloud Heavenly Hues over the blue, making sure to apply a heavy coat in the relief areas of the pot. Wash the brush and blot it dry with paper towel.

4. Using a soft cloth, wipe the excess Heavenly Hues off the pot. Repeat steps 3 and 4 until you are pleased with the end result. Wash the brush and blot it dry with paper towel.

5. Apply a coat of Mod Podge to the inside of the pot and allow it to dry. Wash the foam brush and blot it dry with paper towel.

Stencilled Pot

Instructions:

1. Use the foam paintbrush to apply two to three coats of Sunflower Yellow paint to the outside and bottom of the pot. Allow drying time between each coat. Wash the brush and blot it dry with paper towel.

2. Choose a very simple flower stencil that requires the Fern Green for the leaves and the Foxglove Pink for the petals.

3. Tape the stencil to the side of the pot. Dip the spouncer in the pink paint and apply the paint to the stencil flower in a pouncing motion. Wash the spouncer and blot it dry with paper towel.

4. Repeat step 3 for the leaves, using the Fern Green paint. Allow the paint to dry. Wash the spouncer and blot it dry with paper towel.

5. Repeat steps 3 and 4 to stencil as many flowers on the pot as you wish. Allow the paint to dry.

7. Using the foam paintbrush, apply a coat of Mod Podge to the inside of the pot and allow it to dry. Wash the paintbrush and blot it dry with paper towel.

HINTS, TIPS & GREAT THINGS TO KNOW:

You just can't have enough delightfully decorated flowerpots to enhance your outdoor surroundings. How do you choose the colours? I thought it would be a good idea to coordinate the colours on the flowerpots with the colours in my outdoor furniture. My patio set cushions are a combination of bright pink, yellow, green and blue. I used those same colours on the pots I have around the deck during the summer for a wonderful result.

Patio Placemats

Materials Required:

❖ 4 Fredrix Artists canvas panels 12 x 16 inches (30 cm x 41 cm)
❖ DecoArt Patio Paints:
  1 bottle Sunflower Yellow
  1 bottle Foxglove Pink
  1 bottle Fern Green
  1 bottle Deep Waterfall Blue
  1 bottle Clear Coat

❖ 1 wide-tipped permanent black marker
❖ 1 small foam paintbrush
❖ 1 small piece compressed sponge
❖ water container
❖ paper towel
❖ ruler
❖ pencil
❖ Fiskars 8" Bent Scissors

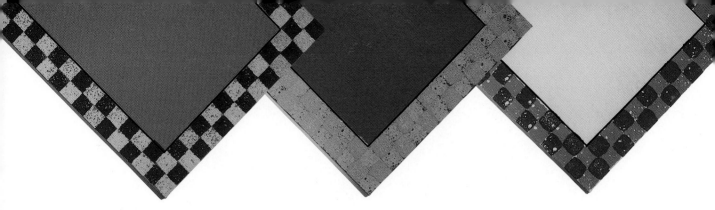

Instructions

1. Using the small foam paintbrush, apply a coat of Sunflower Yellow to the right side of one of the panels. Wash the brush and blot it dry with paper towel.

2. Repeat with the remaining colours, painting each panel a different colour. Allow all paint to dry and apply a second and third coat if necessary. Allow drying time in between coats. Wash the foam paintbrush and blot it dry with paper towel between each colour.

3. Use the ruler and pencil to measure several ¾- x ¾-inch (2-cm x 2-cm) square pieces of compressed sponge. Cut the squares out and place them in water. Once the sponges have expanded, squeeze the excess water out with paper towel.

4. Dip the first sponge into one of the paint colours. On a contrasting colour of panel, sponge two rows of squares, in a checkerboard pattern leaving ¾ inch (2 cm) between each one, all the way around the outside edge of the panel.

5. Repeat step 4 on the other three panels, using contrasting colours of paint and changing sponges as necessary. Allow the paint to dry. Wash all sponges and blot them dry on paper towel.

6. Choose a second contrasting colour for each panel and fill in the blank squares on all panels. Allow all paint to dry thoroughly.

7. Using the ruler and marker, outline the edge of the checkered border pattern between the border and the rest of the panel on each panel, separating the border from the solid area in the middle of the panel. Allow the ink to dry.

8. Use the small foam paintbrush to apply two coats of Clear Coat to the entire surface of each panel to seal the marker, allowing drying time between coats. Let the placemats dry overnight.

HINTS, TIPS & GREAT THINGS TO KNOW:

This is such a simple project, yet so much fun to do. I have incorporated the same colour combinations I used in the clay pot project. The colours blend together well, and I've used Patio Paint again so if the placemats get left out in the rain, no problem.

Backyard Illumination

Glass Votive Holders

These luminaries are so very easy to make, and the results are wonderful. Not only that, you can invite the kids to get involved. Make several large and small, using various sizes of glass bowls for a fabulous effect.

Materials Required:

- ❖ 6 yards (5.5 m) 1-inch (2.5-cm) Offray Sheer Yellow Ribbon
- ❖ 6 round, glass ivy or rose bowls
- ❖ tissue paper in different colours
- ❖ tea lights or votive candles
- ❖ 1 small bottle Plaid Mod Podge gloss
- ❖ 1 small foam paintbrush
- ❖ Fiskars 8" Multi-Purpose Scissors
- ❖ water container
- ❖ paper towel

Instructions:

1. Cut the tissue paper into small pieces in any shape you wish.

2. Use the foam paintbrush to apply a thin coat of the Mod Podge to small areas on the outside of the bowl.

3. Overlap pieces of tissue paper on the outside of the bowl until it is completely covered.

4. Apply two to three coats of podge, allowing it to dry between coats. Wash the paintbrush and blot it dry with paper towel.

5. Insert a tea light or small votive candle.

6. Wrap 1 yard (1 m) of ribbon around the lip of each bowl and tie a shoelace bow.

Those warm, lazy summer evenings inspire me to have some fun decorating the backyard, both for guests and for when my family and I want to relax. Creating subtle lighting out of doors doesn't have to be fancy or costly. You can make funky, fun lighting effects using items you have around the house, or by purchasing everyday items from various sources. I hope these instructions give you lots of great ideas that you can expand on.

Muffin Tin Lighting

This great—and very simple—idea works well both inside and out. If you are using these lights outdoors, you may want to wait for a calm evening, as the candle flame is not protected. Varying the size of the baking tins makes an interesting effect.

Materials Required:

❖ one or more muffin baking tins
❖ votive candles or tea lights in various colours

Instructions:

1. Insert a candle or tea light into each muffin indentation.

Paper Bag Luminaries

Yet another wonderful way to light up the garden path. You can have many paper bag luminaries in a row, lining the front or back path of your home. You can also decorate the outside of the bags before filling them with sand. Because these luminaries are made of paper, though, you will want to keep an eye on them. Using tea lights will keep the flame in check.

Materials Required:

❖ small paper bags
❖ sandbox sand
❖ small tea lights

Instructions:

1. Fold the top edges of each bag over 2".

2. Fill each bag ⅓ full of sand.

3. Insert the tea light into the middle of the sand.

Tin Can Votive Holders

You've probably all heard of this idea, but I can't help passing it along once again as a great idea for outdoor lighting. The shimmering flame flickers through the holes for a dynamite appeal. Purchase several tin cans from the hardware store, or recycle some from around the house. Freezing water in the cans helps them keep their shape while you're working with them. Try using a paper pattern to create a detailed effect.

Materials Required:

- ❖ tin cans in varying sizes
- ❖ pillar candles, votive candles or tea lights
- ❖ water
- ❖ hammer
- ❖ nail
- ❖ paper (optional)
- ❖ tape (optional)

Instructions:

1. Make sure any recycled cans are clean before beginning. Fill cans with water and freeze.

2. If desired, draw a pattern for the holes on paper so you can create the same detailed effect on several cans. Tape the paper in place.

3. Using the hammer and nail, puncture holes through each can using the paper pattern, or punch holes wherever you wish.

4. Replace the ice block with a candle or tea light.

Candles in the Sand

This idea works well for a centrepiece. With the smaller pots, insert one candle and perhaps cover it with a glass hurricane to protect the flame from the wind. You can also use votive or floater candles. Varying the size of the pots and candles adds interest.

Materials Required:

- ❖ clay pots in various sizes
- ❖ sandbox sand
- ❖ one or two glass hurricane lamps (if desired)
- ❖ pillar candles, in varying sizes

Instructions:

1. Pour the sand into the pots, filling to approximately ½ inch (1 cm) from the top.

2. Insert one or more pillar candles into the sand.

3. Cover the pillar candles with a hurricane lamp.

Summer Centrepiece

Materials Required:

- ❖ 1 18-inch (46-cm) moss wreath
- ❖ assortment of Winward Silks flowers:
  12 stems purple Poppies
  8 stems white Gerbers
  5 stems mauve Rose sprays
  3 stems yellow Rose sprays
  4 stems yellow medium Roses
  5 stems small white Daisies
- ❖ 1 4-inch (10-cm) clay pot
- ❖ 1 glass vase or container to protrude from inside the clay pot

- ❖ tea lights
- ❖ DecoArt Patio Paint:
  1 bottle Sunflower Yellow
- ❖ 1 small foam paintbrush
- ❖ Fiskars 8" Bent Scissors
- ❖ water container
- ❖ paper towel
- ❖ Fiskars Craft Snips
- ❖ glue gun and glue sticks

Instructions:

1. Using the foam paintbrush, apply two coats of Sunflower Yellow to the clay pot, inside and out. Allow drying time between each coat. Wash the paintbrush and blot it dry with paper towel.

2. Insert the glass container into the pot and place a tea light in the bottom. Set the pot aside.

3. Using the Craft Snips, cut the stems of all flowers to approximately 2 inches (5 cm) long. If the stems have more than one flower, separate the groupings of flowers into pieces.

4. Insert and glue the poppies around the wreath at even intervals. If you have difficulty inserting the stems into the moss wreath, use scissors to create a hole for the stems to fit into.

5. Repeat step 4 with the gerbers.

6. Insert and glue the pieces of mauve and yellow rose sprays throughout the wreath in a pleasing manner.

7. Fill in with the yellow roses and daisies. The wreath should be completely covered with flowers.

8. Place the clay pot in the middle of the arrangement.

HINTS, TIPS & GREAT THINGS TO KNOW:

You certainly know a wreath when you see it, and traditionally wreaths are hung. However, I decided to turn this wreath into a beautiful flowering centrepiece for the patio or deck. The combination of colours matches my patio decor; you can have a lot of fun mixing and matching flower combinations. Just be sure to incorporate both large and small flowers into your design.

CHAPTER NINE

Holiday Trimmings

Christmas is my favourite time of the year. Some years I have more time than others for decorating and gift making, although I try to do something special each season to add to the decorative items around the house. In this chapter, I have used stars in my decorating plans, so join me as I embark on yet another holiday season with all the trimmings. Make your table festive with stencilled placemats and napkins you can use all year round. Create ornaments and sachets that look fabulous on your tree, or give them as gifts to your dinner guests. Have fun making a holiday wreath that doubles as a centrepiece and try your hand at painting an enchanted candle tray. More importantly, relax and have a great time enjoying the most important people in your life, your friends and family. Have a very merry holiday season, and all the best to you and yours in the new year to come!

Christmas Placemats and Napkins

Materials Required:

- 4 neutral-coloured placemats
- 4 neutral-coloured napkins
- 12 yards (11 m) 2-inch (5-cm) Domcord Belding gold bullion trim
- gold thread
- stencils with various sized star images
- DecoArt Americana Dazzling Metallics:
  1 bottle Venetian Gold
  1 bottle Black Pearl

- 1 small stencil brush
- 1 roll stencil tape
- sewing machine
- straight pins
- Fiskars Softouch Multi-Purpose Scissors
- water container
- paper towel
- iron and ironing board
- pressing cloth

Instructions:

1. Wash and dry all placemats and napkins without using fabric softener or dryer sheets. Press flat.

2. Pin the gold bullion around the edges of each placemat, overlapping the ends slightly. Sew the bullion to the placemats.

3. Tape the largest star stencil in the middle of the right side of one of the place mats.

4. Dip the stencil brush into Venetian Gold paint. Blot the brush on paper towel. Begin applying the paint to the stencil in a pouncing motion, filling in the entire star.

5. Move the stencil to the top right corner and stencil one large gold star. Repeat in the bottom left corner.

6. Stencil smaller stars in between the larger ones. Wash the stencils and stencil brush and blot them dry on paper towel.

7. Repeat the same process with Black Pearl paint, using only the smaller star images until you are satisfied with the pattern. Allow all paint to dry. Wash the stencil and stencil brush and blot them dry on paper towel.

8. Repeat steps 3 to 7 on all four placemats.

9. Repeat the same process on the right side of the four napkins, stencilling small star images in the corners of the napkins only. Allow all paint to dry. Wash the stencil and stencil brush and blot them dry on paper towel.

10. Set the iron on high. Turn the placemats and napkins face down. Place a pressing cloth on the back of the placemats and napkins. Press with the hot iron to heat set the paint. Allow the linens to cure for 72 hours before washing.

HINTS, TIPS & GREAT THINGS TO KNOW:

You don't have to be a sewer or an artist to make these wonderful holiday placemats and coordinating napkins. In fact, you don't even have to reserve these beautiful table items for Christmas. Take them out and show them off to guests any time of the year. What I love about this project is you start with finished placemats and napkins. All you do is the decorating. Use glazes, acrylic paints or fabric paints to achieve the same result. Just make sure you add a textile medium to the acrylic paint or heat set the items after they are finished by pressing them with a hot iron on the reverse side of the painted design. This process will allow you to wash and dry your table linens without worrying about fading. For an added touch, make soft napkin holders out of wired cording and tassels.

Sachet Pillows

Materials Required
(to make 3 to 4 pillows):

- ¼ yard (0.2 m) each of three different fabrics, such as moire
- 3 to 5 yards (2.75 m to 4.5 m) various Offray 1½-inch (4-cm) ribbon
- 1 small bottle potpourri oil
- 1 bag polyester fibrefill
- sewing needle
- thread
- straight pins
- Fiskars Softouch Multi-Purpose Scissors
- measuring tape
- sewing machine

HINTS, TIPS & GREAT THINGS TO KNOW:

It's so nice to be able to present your guests with some kind of small gift when they sit down at the holiday table. There are many great ideas. I thought these little sachet pillows were a great gift idea and something your guests will find useful after the season has ended. I have used various types of fabrics; however, you can also make these any size, using various widths of ribbon. If you are not a sewer, you could get away with using fabric glue.

Instructions:

1. Using one of the three fabrics chosen, measure and cut four pieces approximately 5 x 5 inches (12.5 cm x 12.5 cm) each.

2. With right sides together, pin two of the pieces together, leaving a 2-inch (5-cm) opening on one side.

3. Sew each pair together leaving a ½-inch (1-cm) seam allowance. Clip all corners. Turn each pillow right side out and adjust all corners.

4. Stuff both pillows firmly with the polyester fibrefill. Pin and hand sew the opening closed on both pillows.

5. Cut a piece of ribbon 1 yard (1 m) in length. Place one pillow on top of the other.

6. Wrap the ribbon from top to bottom on the pillows as you would wrap a gift. Cross the ribbon underneath and bring it back up to meet at the top of the pillows. Tie a knot and a shoelace bow.

7. Using your finger, dab a very small amount of the potpourri oil onto the middle of the bow. Be careful not to mark the ribbon with the oil.

8. Repeat steps 1 to 7 with the rest of the fabrics and ribbons.

Holiday Candle Tray

Materials Required:

- 1 Walnut Hollow 12- x 16-inch (30-cm x 41-cm) rectangle tray
- DecoArt Americana acrylic paints:
  1 bottle Buttermilk
  1 bottle Lamp Ebony Black
- DecoArt Dazzling Metallics:
  1 bottle Glorious Gold
  1 bottle Bronze
- 1 bottle DecoArt Faux Glazing Medium

- 1 small bottle matte acrylic varnish
- Plaid Decorator Blocks stars
- several sizes of pillar candles
- 2 small foam paintbrushes
- 1 small flat paintbrush
- fine grit sandpaper
- paper towel
- water container

Instructions:

1. Sand the tray well and wipe any dust particles away with damp paper towel.

2. Using one of the small foam paintbrushes, apply two to three coats of Buttermilk paint, allowing drying time between each coat. Wash the paintbrush and blot it dry on paper towel.

3. Decide on the pattern you wish for the top of the tray. You can create a star motif on the inside or around the rim of the tray.

4. Mix the Lamp Ebony Black paint with the Faux Glazing Medium to create a glaze. The ratio should be 50:50.

5. Apply the glaze to the star blocks with the small flat paintbrush and print stars according to the manufacturer's instructions.

Take into account you are going to be block printing gold or bronze stars as well, so leave enough space in between the black stars. Wash the blocks and brush and blot them dry with paper towel.

6. Repeat steps 4 and 5 with the gold or bronze paint, or both. Block print more stars onto the tray. Allow all glaze to dry. Wash the blocks and brush and blot them dry with paper towel.

7. With the second foam paintbrush, apply two to three coats of the acrylic varnish, allowing drying time between each coat. Wash the paintbrush and blot it dry on paper towel.

8. Enhance the tray with an assortment of pillar candles.

HINTS, TIPS & GREAT THINGS TO KNOW:

Trays have many functions, and can be used for other than carrying items back and forth from the kitchen. I love the idea of placing things like candles, beads and potpourri on beautifully decorated trays for a wonderful accent to any home decor theme. This tray can be displayed throughout the year.

Christmas Wreath Centrepiece

Materials Required:

❖ 1 36-inch (91-cm) PVC greenery wreath
❖ assortment of Winward Silks flowers:
  6 stems white glittered Peonies
  3 stems white glittered Hydrangea
  5 stems cream Queen Anne's Lace
  6 stems white berries
❖ 4 yards (3.7 m) Domcord Belding cream and gold cording
❖ 4 Domcord Belding cream and gold tassels
❖ 1 large three-wick cream pillar candle
❖ Fiskars 8" Bent Scissors
❖ glue gun and glue sticks
❖ Fiskars Craft Snips

Instructions:

1. Open the wreath up and "fluff" it by moving the pieces of greenery around.

2. Using the craft snips, cut the stems of the peonies so they're approximately 3 inches (8 cm) long. Remove all the leaves from the stems and set aside.

3. Repeat step 2 for the hydrangea, cutting the flower into smaller pieces and setting aside the leaves.

4. Remove the stems from the Queen Anne's lace and cut each flower into two pieces.

5. Cut the berries apart so there are approximately four pieces per stem.

6. Insert and glue the peonies around the wreath at regular intervals.

7. Insert and glue the leaves of the peonies around each flower.

8. Insert and glue small pieces of hydrangea around the peonies and in any open areas.

9. Insert and glue the pieces of Queen Anne's lace to fill in the open areas.

10. Arrange the leaves from the hydrangea stems in and around the various flowers in the wreath. Glue in place.

11. Glue the pieces of berries throughout the arrangement.

12. Loop the cording through the wreath, using the boughs of the wreath to hold it in place.

13. Attach the tassels to four evenly spaced areas of the cording by using a slipknot on each tassel.

14. Place the large three-wick candle in the middle of the design.

HINTS, TIPS & GREAT THINGS TO KNOW:

Here's one more way to use a greenery wreath, other than hanging it on your door. You can choose any size of wreath you wish, and adjust the amount of flowers needed to complete the project. Change the colours and make the centrepiece using burgundy flowers, or mix cream with burgundy.

Frosted Keepsake Ornaments

Materials Required:

- 6 medium clear Christmas ball ornaments
- 1 small bottle Armour Etch glass etching cream
- 1 package iridescent shred
- 6 yards (5.5 m) Offray Cream Spool O' Ribbon
- 3 packages acid-free star stickers
- 1 gold paint pen
- 1 silver paint pen
- 1 bottle gold dimensional fabric paint
- 1 bottle silver dimensional fabric paint
- 1 bottle fine gold glitter
- 1 bottle fine iridescent glitter
- Fiskars 8" Multi-Purpose Scissors
- 1 small foam paintbrush
- 1 pair disposable latex gloves
- water container
- paper towel

HINTS, TIPS & GREAT THINGS TO KNOW:

These beautiful Christmas ornaments are made using two different methods. You can combine dimensional paint with glitter to create a real sparkle, or simply use the gold and silver paint pens for a subtle look. Either way, these ornaments are a wonderful addition to any holiday decorating, or a well-received Christmas gift.

Instructions:

1. Remove the top from all of the ornaments.

2. Place approximately 12 stickers on each glass ball. Be sure to use acid-free stickers given the strength of the etching cream.

3. Wearing the disposable latex gloves, use the paintbrush to cover the first ball entirely with a thick coat of the etching cream. Allow the cream to sit on the ball for 2 minutes and rinse with cold water to remove the cream. Allow the ball to dry thoroughly. Repeat this process for the other five ornaments. Discard brush.

4. Remove the stickers to reveal a pattern of clear star images. On two ornaments, outline the images with a combination of the paint pens, alternating the gold and the silver. Choose other squiggle patterns to complete the look.

5. On two other ornaments, outline half the stars with the gold dimensional fabric paint. While the paint is still wet, sprinkle the painted surface with gold glitter. Repeat with the silver paint and the iridescent glitter on the remaining stars. Allow the ornaments to dry.

6. On the remaining ornaments, combine the methods in steps 4 and 5.

7. Fill each ornament with the iridescent shred and replace the top.

8. Tie each ornament with 1 yard (1 m) of ribbon to hang them on the tree.

DecoArt
P.O. Box 386,
Stanford, KY 40484
Phone: (606) 365-3193
Fax: (606) 365-9739
Website: www.decoart.com

Designer Fabric Outlet
1360 Queen Street West,
Toronto, Ontario, Canada
M6K 1L7
Phone: (416) 531-2810 or (416) 531-3796
Fax: (416) 531-4114

Domcord Belding
660 Denison Street,
Markham, Ontario, Canada
L3R 1C1
Fax only: (905) 475-7022
Website: www.domcord.com

Fiskars Canada, Inc.
201 Whitehall Drive, #1
Markham, Ontario, Canada
L3R 9Y3
Phone: (905) 940-8460
Toll Free: 1-800-488-5029
Fax: (905) 940-8469
Website: www.fiskars.com

Offray Ribbon Canada Inc.
433 Chabanel St. West, Suite 205
Montreal, Quebec, Canada
H2N 2J3
Phone: (514) 858-7073
Toll Free: 1-800-363-3729
Fax: (514) 858-7076
Website: www.offray.com

SaMi's Custom Window Coverings
Sandra Nash Design Consultant
2297 Grand Ravine Drive,
Oakville, Ontario, Canada
L6H 6A8
Phone: (905) 257-5755
Fax: (905) 257-2075

Walnut Hollow
1409 State Road 23,
Dodgeville, WI 53533-2112
Toll Free: 1-800-950-5101
Fax: (608) 935-7511
Website: www.walnuthollow.com
E-mail: walnut@walnuthollow.com

Winward Silks of Canada Inc.
6225 Danville Road,
Mississauga, Ontario, Canada
L5T 2H7
Phone: (905) 670-0888
Fax: (905) 670-8848
Toll Free Fax: 1-888-946-9273 (Canada only)
Website: www.winwardsilks.com
E-mail: info@winwardcanada.com

Sue Warden Visualmedia Inc.
200 North Service Road West,
Unit 1, Suite 355
Oakville, Ontario, Canada
L6M 2Y1
Fax: (905) 847-8958
Website: www.suewarden.com
E-mail: swarden@suewarden.com

The Kitchen p. 6

Dinner plate/bowl
Festival Yellow dinnerware set: Pier 1 Imports

Olive green waffle weave towel: Pier 1 Imports

Glasses
365± glasses 36 cl 12 pk: IKEA

Harlequin Recipe Box p. 20

Herb plant: Sheridan Nurseries

Placemats with a Twist p. 23

Bowl/dinner plate/cup and saucer
Festival Yellow dinnerware: Pier 1 Imports

Mosaic Utensil Container p. 31

Bowl
Festival Yellow dinnerware: Pier 1 Imports

The Dining Room p. 32

Plates
Minuskel 20 pc dinner set: IKEA

Wine glasses
Ripple wine glasses: Pier 1 Imports

The Family Room p. 46

Table lamp
Tunna table lamp
Millerit dark green shade: IKEA

Stencilled Side Tables p. 50

Glasses
365± glasses 36 cl 12 pk: IKEA

Table lamp
Tunna table lamp
Millerit dark green shade: IKEA

The Powder Room p. 62

Perfume bottles: Pier 1 Imports

Blue Towels
Bay blue Tommy Hilfiger
face cloth/hand towels: Eaton's

Pink towels
Royal velvet capri towels: Eaton's

The Master Bedroom p. 74

Pillow on chair
17" x 17" Bay of Bengel pillow: Eaton's

Black and beige throw pillow on bed
Faux silk pillow 12" x 17": Eaton's

Black King pillowcases: Eaton's

The Children's Bedroom p. 88

Cactus: Sheridan Nurseries

Pots, Pots and More Pots p. 116

Murtle topiary: Sheridan Nurseries

Patio Placemats p. 119

Dinnerplate/bowl
Festival Yellow dinnerware: Pier 1 Imports

Flatware
Lilly 5 pc setting: Pier 1 Imports

Yellow napkin: Pier 1 Imports

Christmas Placemats and Napkins p. 128

Glass bowl with gold rim: Pier 1 Imports

Candles
Fenomen block candles
20 cm/15 cm/10 cm: IKEA

Frosted Keepsake Ornaments p. 136

Glass bowl with gold rim: Pier 1 Imports

Index